Praise for

The Yearning Soul

"*The Yearning Soul* beautifully portrays the panorama of our eternal existence, as revealed through the Prophet Joseph Smith. The book both inspires and gives hope as it lays out the eternal truths behind our divine identities as children of a loving and relatable Heavenly Father."

—**Gary E. Smith,** LDS painter and artist

"*The Yearning Soul* is a journey worth taking into the beautiful truths of the restored gospel and how they answer so many of the great questions of life, especially those posed by questioning souls."

—**Larry W. Peterson,** managing editor of the Dr. Hyrum L. Andrus Project (www.HyrumAndrus.com)

"In an elegant style, *The Yearning Soul* unearths the revealed knowledge of our divine destinies and identities by exploring the core truths of the restored gospel. It is a wonderful and inspiring read."

—**Brett A. Folkman,** doctor of ministry

The Yearning SOUL

The Yearning SOUL

UNEARTHING *your* DIVINE DESTINY

DAVID OLSEN

CFI
An Imprint of Cedar Fort, Inc.
Springville, Utah

This is not an official publication of The Church of Jesus Christ of Latter-day Saints. The opinions and views expressed herein belong solely to the author and do not necessarily represent the opinions or views of Cedar Fort, Inc. Permission for the use of sources, graphics, and photos is also solely the responsibility of the author.

ISBN 13: 978-1-4621-1722-2

Published by CFI, an imprint of Cedar Fort, Inc.
2373 W. 700 S., Springville, UT 84663
Distributed by Cedar Fort, Inc., www.cedarfort.com

LIBRARY OF CONGRESS CATALOGING-IN-PUBLICATION DATA

Olsen, David, author.
The yearning soul : unearthing your divine destiny / David Olsen.
pages cm
Includes bibliographical references.
ISBN 978-1-4621-1722-2 (perfect bound : alk. paper)
1. Christian life--Mormon authors. 2. Church of Jesus Christ of Latter-day Saints--Doctrines. 3. Mormon Church--Doctrines. I. Title.

BX8656.O5185 2015
248.4'893--dc23

2015032940

Cover design by Shawnda T. Craig

Edited and typeset by Kevin Haws

Printed in the United States of America

10 9 8 7 6 5 4 3 2 1

Printed on acid-free paper

Just as President Wilford Woodruff compared Joseph Smith to "a bed of gold, concealed from human view" (as quoted by John Longden, in Conference Report, April 1959, 34–36), I dedicate this book to Dr. Hyrum L. Andrus, a gospel scholar of the past whose writings deserve to be unearthed and read by a new generation of the Church.

Contents

Contents

Introduction: A Letter from an Old Friend

Brett,[1] this book is for you. It has been several years since we have seen each other, but you have been on my mind of late.

Since being released as your bishop, I have learned that you are not engaged in living the gospel.

The chapters that follow have been written with you in mind. Think of this book as an invitation for you to take a second look at the meaningful truths of the restored gospel of Jesus Christ and how they answer many of the great questions of life.

I want to take you on a journey similar to that of C. S. Lewis, the once-atheist who became the great Christian writer. Through his friendship with J. R. R. Tolkien, the author of *The Lord of the Rings* and a devout Catholic, Lewis reexamined his life as an atheist and found Christ.

C. S. Lewis had Tolkien as a human guide and intellectual equal. I desire for you to receive the same insights and walk down the same spiritual path that Lewis traveled—the path that firmly entrenched his belief in Christ as the source of truth, purpose, and meaning. I desire to have similar open and honest conversations with you, relating to the teachings and principles of the LDS Church.

President Thomas S. Monson declared, "There is no need for you or for me, in this enlightened age when the fulness of the gospel has been restored, to sail uncharted seas or to travel unmarked roads in search of truth. A loving Heavenly Father has plotted our course and provided an unfailing guide."[2]

Serving as your bishop, I knew you were a gifted young man. I enjoyed the times we met for lunch to talk about your questions. It was apparent that you were given to deep reflection and truth-seeking. I remember thinking, *Here is a young man "trailing clouds of glory,"*[3] to borrow a well-worn phrase from Wordsworth.

I knew that you brought something special with you from our premortal existence. People don't often write the poetry you wrote or compose the classical music you composed at such a young age. It takes the rest of us years to develop talents like yours. When you shared your poetry with me, it reminded me of a poem from gospel scholar and academic Hugh Nibley (whose work you would greatly enjoy). Nibley wrote these lines when he was seventeen: "A last farewell of dizzy, mottled strain. . . . A glimmer, half of thought and half of sight—a blue-white glimmer in a hole-black void. . . . Catches my last retreating sense—'tis vega!"[4]

When I read those words recently, I thought of you and your life of promise and destiny under Heavenly Father's watchful gaze.

So this book is written for you and others like you, who are searching for knowledge and truth, but perhaps the gospel teaching of your youth did not fill you with the deep and penetrating philosophical insights that the gospel can bring into a person's life.

I hope this book will rekindle the Light of Christ that you need to give you the flashes of insight of your divine potential and sense of your destiny as a child of God.

I thank you in advance for your time and your intellectual honesty in considering the principles and truths that have profoundly affected my life.

Your friend eternally,
David P. Olsen

Chapter 1
C. S. Lewis: From Atheist to Christian

"I believe in Christianity as I believe that the sun has risen. Not only because I see it, but because by it I see everything else."[5]

How can I know there is a God? Is that God reaching out to me patiently and lovingly?

An earthquake in a small region in Armenia devastated a city. A father ran quickly to his son's school. Reaching the structure—now a pile of rubble—he frantically (yet carefully) began to remove the broken pieces of the building. There were no signs of life.

When others told him to stop because it was hopeless, he said he had made a promise to his son that no matter what he would always be there. He continued to remove the rubble from where he estimated his son's classroom had been. Other parents cried and wailed but did not help him.

Alone, he removed rubble for thirty-eight hours when he heard voices from within the ruins of the school. "Armand," he screamed.

"Dad, it's me . . . Armand," his son replied. Then the father heard him say, "I told the other kids not to worry. I told them that if you were alive, you'd save me, and when you saved me, they'd be saved. You promised you would always be there for me. You did it, Dad!"

The father helped his son and thirteen other boys and girls from the debris.[6]

Is there a God, a kind and generous Heavenly Father who patiently and lovingly searches through the rubble of our lives, hoping to bring us home?

C. S. Lewis: From Atheist to Christian

Known later in his life as a great Christian intellectual and writer, C. S. Lewis's writings on the nature of the Atonement, the hope of redemption that Christ holds out to fallen humanity, and the sweet promises of joy in resurrection, in life after death, have touched the lives of millions of people. However, for most of his life, Lewis was an atheist.

Through a series of events, Heavenly Father—through Christ—reached out patiently and lovingly to Lewis, similar to the Armenian father searching for his son in the rubble. Heavenly Father sifted through the rubble of Lewis's life and would not stop until He reached his son.

As a child, Lewis was awed by the wonder and beauty of nature around his home in the lush Irish countryside. Imaginative from a young age, he and his older brother, Warnie, would hide away in a wardrobe and imagine stories with mythical creatures and anthropomorphic animals in a magical land called Boxen.

But the happiness of Lewis's childhood ended tragically when his mother died from cancer when he was ten years old. Shortly thereafter, he was sent to a miserable boarding school, where the schoolmaster was soon committed to a psychiatric hospital. Later, Lewis was afflicted with respiratory problems and was sent away from his family to live in another town. There, he attended the preparatory school Cherbourg House. It was during this time that he rejected his Christian beliefs and became an atheist.

Lewis's atheism became further entrenched as he served on the front lines during World War I in the Somme Valley in France. The threat of death was real and close as the war took young and promising lives away from this world. On his nineteenth birthday, Lewis experienced trench warfare for the first time. He was later wounded by a British shell that missed its target and killed two of his fellow soldiers. He reported stepping into the dark, soul-crushing pit of depression as he recovered in an army hospital.

Lewis was a brilliant young man. After the war, he returned to Oxford University, where he mastered Greek, Latin, and other ancient languages, as well as philosophy and English literature. He loved ancient myths. For Lewis at this time in his life, a belief in the Christian God was just as valid as a belief in the gods of myth and legend, like Prometheus or Cyrus.

Along with J. R. R. Tolkien, who was also enamored with myth and the ancient world, Lewis served on the English faculty at Oxford. Tolkien and Lewis became friends and would take long walks into the woods and discuss religion and philosophy. Tolkien, a devout Catholic, challenged Lewis that Christianity was the true myth to which other myths pointed—that Christ is all of those myths incarnate and that this pattern of belief and worship through mankind's history was not accidental. Many of those myths described a god or gods who died in a sacrifice for their people, and then the god or gods resurrected into new bodies full of glory. Lewis would argue back that Christianity contained some elements of truth but was scarcely original.[7]

Tolkien continued to debate with Lewis over the years. Lewis, an honest intellectual, later remarked that as he talked with Tolkien he felt his atheistic constructs beginning to give way. He eventually became a deist, believing that a creator exists but that a supreme being does not intervene in the workings of the universe, let alone in the lives of everyday people.

Then a significant event occurred: Lewis's father passed away. Since the death of his mother, Lewis had an estranged relationship with his father. But after his father's passing, Lewis could feel his father's presence. He called this a supernatural experience that he could not explain. Reluctantly, at thirty-two years old, Lewis reaffiliated himself with the Anglican community. In his words, he became "a very ordinary layman of the Church of England."[8]

Over the next several years, Lewis came to slowly know Christ in an intimate way. He remarked that he was "feeling the unrelenting approach of him who I so earnestly desired not to meet."[9] He described the process as if it was being thrust upon him. He fought against it intellectually; he said of his conversion, "It came up from behind and took over my heart."[10] He could sense that something was happening to him and that he was caught in the flow of the experience. Earlier, when some of his atheist friends had converted to Christianity, he felt they were weak-minded, giving into emotionalism. Now, he found himself undergoing the same transformation. Needless to say, Lewis went from being the self-proclaimed "most reluctant convert in England"[11] to a staunch advocate and defender of Christianity.

Lewis referred to this rebirth into Christianity as the process of the old self needing to die. This was a theme through much of his writing. For example, in his book *The Voyage of the Dawn Treader*, the arrogant young boy Eustace becomes a dragon, symbolizing his fallen mortal nature. The boy does not like being a dragon and unsuccessfully tries to tear at his dragon skin. Then Aslan, a literary figure of Christ, steps forward and says that only he can tear off the skin and turn Eustace into a new creature.[12] This beautifully teaches that we need to surrender to Christ to receive His help to be transformed into our true selves.

Lewis understood the Atonement and gave meaning to these life-giving, rejuvenating powers. In his book *The Great Divorce*, a red lizard sits on a spirit's shoulder, whispering lustful things that the spirit enjoyed. An angel approaches and asks for the spirit's permission to kill the lizard. The spirit, in effect, responds, "We don't need to go that far and kill the lizard. I occasionally like to entertain those lustful thoughts." Eventually, the spirit gives the angel permission to kill the lizard. After the lizard dies, it turns into a beautiful black stallion for the spirit to ride.[13] Lewis's message was to give up certain things to follow Christ and He will come into your life in profound ways. But the choice is always ours.

This Book Is Not about C. S. Lewis—It Is about You

The chapters that follow have been written with you in mind, as an invitation to take a second look at the meaningful truths of the restored gospel of Jesus Christ and how they answer many of the great questions of life.

As you read this book, you need to know two things. One, Heavenly Father knows you personally—actually better than you know yourself. Two, like the Armenian father, Heavenly Father is reaching out to you in His own ways, even right now as you read this book.

You ask, "How is this true? If He is all powerful, why hasn't he reached out to me in more profound ways so I know with certainty that He exists?"

The answer is your sincere, honest, and open search for Heavenly Father and your questions about your existence are essential in this world where we must walk by faith. This journey is important for realizing your identity as a daughter or son of God. You must know more than just God exists. He desires most to have a relationship with you and for you to experience Him through revelation and reason.

For this book to be meaningful and touch your soul, you need to know that God knows you personally. I was in a Church meeting once where the following story was relayed:

Joseph Millett, with his large family, was suffering through very, very difficult times. He wrote in his journal:

> One of my children came in and said that Brother Newton Hall's folks was out of bread, had none that day.
>
> I divided our flour in a sack to send up to Brother Hall. Just then Brother Hall came.
>
> Says I, "Brother Hall, are you out of flour?"
>
> "Brother Millett, we have none."
>
> "Well, Brother Hall, there is some in that sack. I have divided and was going to send it to you. Your children told mine that you was out."
>
> Brother Hall began to cry. He said he had tried others, but could not get any. He went to the cedars and prayed to the Lord, and the Lord told him to go to Joseph Millett.
>
> "Well Brother Hall, you needn't bring this back. If the Lord sent you for it you don't owe me for it."
>
> That night Joseph Millett recorded a remarkable sentence in his journal:
>
> "You can't tell me how good it made me feel to know that the Lord knew there was such a person as Joseph Millett."[14]

The Lord knows Joseph Millett and He knows you and me.

After the meeting where I heard that story, a man I did not know well approached me. He asked if we could talk privately. We stepped away to a quiet place. "I have a problem," the man said. "I've been praying for a solution, and every time I pray, I am directed to come find you because you can help me solve it."

I took him to lunch the next day, and we started to work toward solutions. But as I drove home that night, I was filled with the marvelous manifestation of love and recognition that Heavenly Father knew me well enough to know that I could help this man. I echo emphatically with Joseph Millett, "You can't tell me how good it made me feel to know that the Lord knew there was such a person as Joseph Millett."

Truth-Seeking and the Great Questions of Life

There are many great questions of spiritual significance in life. The aim of this book is to answer these questions, not for you but with you.

Is there a supreme being who created you and me? Am I being intellectually authentic by accepting or rejecting a belief in God? Have I had experiences with God that I may have dismissed as emotions gone awry? Am I open to discovering new truth? If the existence of a supreme being is at all possible, is it important to understand my relationship with this being?

To end the chapter, I want to share a few thoughts from C. S. Lewis on reason and truth-seeking, as well as imagination to capture a vision of reality and its meaning. First off, C. S. Lewis believed that Heavenly Father made us for joy.[15] "God is the great "hedonist,"[16] he once wrote. For Heavenly Father, happiness is the object and design of our existence.[17]

Lewis also believed that mankind has been endowed with powers of perception and reason by God. He viewed our powers of reason as the God-given "organ of truth" and imagination as the "organ of meaning." For Lewis, imagination acted as a cosmic pointer to God.[18]

Case in point: One day as an unbeliever, C. S. Lewis was traveling by train and bought the book *Phantastes* by Christian writer George MacDonald. As he read, he reported that a "new quality" touched him and his imagination was "baptized." He later recognized the new quality as holiness. He also said that it took a while for the rest of him to catch up.[19]

As an honest truth seeker, accepting truth in all its shades and hues of good and evil, C. S. Lewis said of the experience of gaining new spiritual insights,

> "Look out!" we cry, "it's *alive*." And therefore this is the very point at which so many draw back—I would have done so myself if I could—and proceed no further with Christianity. An "impersonal God"—well

> and good. A subjective God of beauty, truth, and goodness, inside our own heads—better still. A formless life-force surging through us, a vast power which we can tap—best of all. But God Himself, alive, pulling at the other end of the cord, perhaps approaching at an infinite speed, the hunter, king, husband—that is quite another matter.[20]

At another time, C. S. Lewis wrote, "God cannot give us a happiness and peace apart from Himself, because it is not there. There is no such thing. . . . Christianity, if false, is of no importance, and if true, of infinite importance. The only thing it cannot be is moderately important."[21]

Like this book, C. S. Lewis wrestled with many ideas, not just through reason and imagination but also literature, myth, philosophy, art, and more. For him, all this truth-seeking pointed to the source of light and truth: the Son of God who, modern-day revelation teaches us, "ascended up on high, as also he descended below all things, in that he comprehended all things, that he might be in all and through all things, the light of truth" (D&C 88:6).

The Purpose of This Book

This book is intended to help you discover the true natures of your Father in Heaven and Christ. I want to be your Tolkien as we walk through the still and quietness of the woods of discovery. In this book, I have tried to explain who our Heavenly Father is as a tender-hearted Man of Holiness, ever reaching out to us, inviting us to become like Him. Through His spiritual powers, He is connected with everything in His vast creations. Not a sparrow falls that He is unaware of.

I have tried to explain who Christ is to us: our Redeemer, Savior, companion, and friend. Think of a being such as Christ. The radiance of His spirit is brighter than the sun at noonday.

We will walk through your existence prior to the formation of your spirit body, through premortality, and into this fallen mortal sphere. I hope to explain to you the meaning of life in this mortal sphere and what lies beyond in our future, glorified, resurrected state.

As you read, listen to Father in Heaven and discover what His plan is for you.

Happy reading!

Chapter 2
Life Is a Mysterious Gift

"When the first self submits to the deeper self, they are reconciled and walk on together."[22]

What is the meaning of my life? Who am I? Is my identity preceding this mortal experience eternal?

Life Is a Gift—A Mysterious Gift . . .

In what is now modern-day Iraq, Gilgamesh, king of Uruk, wrote an epic poem in 2,000 BC in which he lamented the death of his friend Enkidu. The poem is considered one of the first great works of literature.[23]

As Gilgamesh mourned the loss of his dear friend, he became preoccupied with death and questions of the meaning of life and his own mortality. Unable to find solace, Gilgamesh set out on a mythic journey to seek an audience with Utnapishtim, the god who holds the secret of eternal life.

The journey was difficult physically, psychological, and spiritually. He endured poisonous scorpions, climbed a great mountain in cold and darkness, and sailed on a raft across the sea. Gilgamesh was not so much seeking eternal life, but rather desired to extend his life in this mortal sphere. In the poem, Gilgamesh poignantly described over and over his intense desire to keep on living and not face the void of death.

He then met Siduri, a girl who provided life-saving drinks to travelers. Gilgamesh rehearsed his story of grief and the loss of his dear friend and asked for directions to Utnapishtim. Next, he met Urshanabi, a ferryman of sorts who directed him on how to reach Utnapishtim. Gilgamesh, still feeling his deep grief, said, "Mortality reached him [Enkidu] first and I am left this week to weep and wail for his shriveling corpse which scares me. Won't I soon be like him, stone cold and dead, for all days to come?"[24]

Urshanabi and Gilgamish built a raft and sailed to meet the god Utnapishtim. Upon meeting the god, Gilgamesh collapsed from exhaustion. When Gilgamesh awoke, Utnapishtim complimented him for his fortitude, displayed during his quest for truth and knowledge.

Utnapishtim said,

> Gilgamesh! You labored much to come here.
> How can I reward you for traveling back?
> May I share a special secret, one that the gods alone do know?
> There is a plant that hides somewhere among the rocks that thirsts
> and thrusts itself deep in the earth, with thistles that sting.
> That plant contains eternal life for you.[25]

Gilgamesh dove into cold waters and found the plant. It stung him, but he brought it to the surface. He resolved to bring the plant back to his kingdom, where he would give it to "aged men as food" and "eat it and to be made forever young." But on his journey home while Gilgamesh swam in a pool of water, a snake slithered along and stole the plant, dashing Gilgamesh's hopes for immortality. In despair, he watches the snake grow young.

Returning to his kingdom in Uruk, Gilgamesh looked upon the city with new eyes. The walls of the city held special significance for him. Through his journey of personal discovery, he became a new person, with a newfound awareness of himself and the mystery of his being. Gilgamesh learned that life holds deeper meaning than he had heretofore supposed.

The Mystery of Your Being

On his journey, Gilgamesh learned something about the mystery of his being and the need to live authentically and honestly here in mortality. Lord Byron, the romantic poet, mused, "Let me but be taught the mystery of my being."[26] The poet John Keats penned that we are "straining at particles of light in the midst of a great darkness."[27] And the Apostle Paul wrote about our perceptions in life, that "we see through a glass, darkly" (1 Corinthians 13:12).

Yet it is with the knowledge of the restored gospel that we can see things of this life clearly and know the mystery of our being.

Like Gilgamesh, throughout history daughters and sons of God have been searching to peer behind the veil of this existence and understand the mystery of their beings—what lies beyond after they die.

In a spiritual quest, the pharaohs of Egypt built cavernous pyramids to entomb themselves and devised elaborate means of navigating the afterlife, even burying their servants alive with them to help the pharaohs on their mystical journey. Qin Shi Huang, first emperor of China, commissioned the Terracotta Army. The purpose of these replicas of Huang's real-life army was to protect him in the afterlife. Stonehenge is believed to be a place of pilgrimage and burial ground, dating to as early as 3,000 BC, and some archeologists believe the massive pillars are aligned perfectly to gaze into the night skies for astrological purposes. In our day, we spend billions of dollars exploring the tiniest parts of antimatter and build better and better telescopes to peer into the farthest reaches of the galaxy, searching for distant signs of life.

President Thomas S. Monson said, "Throughout the ages, men and women have sought for knowledge and understanding concerning this mortal existence and their place and purpose in it, as well as for the way to peace and happiness. Such a search is undertaken by each of us. This knowledge and understanding are available to all mankind. They are contained in truths which are eternal." He then quoted John Jaques' hymn *Oh Say What is Truth*, proclaiming, "Tho the heavens depart and the earth's fountains burst, / Truth, the sum of existence, will weather the worst, / Eternal, unchanged, evermore."[28]

By coming to know Christ intimately and personally, you learn something of the eternal and the mystery of your being. One of the purposes of this book is to help you learn the mystery of your true being.

Know Thyself

We are mysteries to ourselves; inherently, we do not know who we are or where we come from. We are born into this world as helpless infants and, through experience, we come into our own, searching for meaning and understanding. For this reason, the Greeks, on the forecourt of the Temple of Apollo at Delphi, inscribed the words *know thyself.*

Yet as we live our lives, we are a mystery to be revealed to ourselves.

One of the great purposes of life is to unearth our true identities as daughters and sons of God—all of this is purposeful as the work and glory of a loving Heavenly Father (see Moses 1:39). Through life, we experience the world through our senses. We see the beauty and wonder of the setting sun over blue oceans. We hear the majesty of a symphony or the whispered hush of a mother's love. We smell the fragrance of nature carried on a summer wind. We touch the tactile wonders of the world. We love and feel loved and yearn to be more than we are. Yet we have feelings that we are strangers here, that we don't quiet belong to this temporal sphere.

We are like Adam after rising from the dust and finding himself alone in the Garden of Eden after the Creation. With a veil of forgetfulness gently placed across his brow, Adam could well have asked, "Where am I? How did I get here?" But his larger question (and the one that we must also answer ourselves) may have been, "Who am I?"

We too have the same questions about our existence. These questions are purposeful on Heavenly Father's part. The longing for answers pushes us to search for meaning and ultimately revealed knowledge about the path back to His joy-filled and glorious presence.

What is behind this frail, mortal, and sometimes confusing experience, through which we walk by faith? Is it Heavenly Father, encouraging us to become more like Him? Are we molded from God's express image? Why has Heavenly Father implanted within us His divine nature that needs to be developed in a fallen world? Does His heart ache for us to live His way and bestow upon us eternal life so we can live a more abundant and happier lives here and in the eternities? Will we one day have bodies like His, filled with light and truth so that we may also shine above the brightness of the sun?

These are the questions this book strives to answer. We chose to come here to earth to become more like Heavenly Father and Christ, to pass though this veil of tears and experience the joy and goodness of man. As we beheld Father in Heaven's supreme goodness, majesty, and glory, we desired to receive such an immortal body, filled with light, truth, beauty, goodness, and intelligence. That opportunity caused us to shout with joy. We understood that by receiving a mortal body, we could one day be filled with the joy, light, and intelligence of our Heavenly Father. As we read in Doctrine and Covenants 88:67, "If your eye be single to my glory, your whole bodies shall be filled with light, and there shall be no darkness in you; and that body which is filled with light comprehendeth all things."

Walk with me in the following chapters as I do my best to explain the mystery of our beings, as revealed through the light of the restored gospel.

Chapter 3
The Desire for Light and Truth

"The larger the island of knowledge, the
longer the shoreline of wonder."[29]

What drives mankind's quest for progress? How can a person know God exists? Why did He create me with all these yearnings to understand myself and fulfill my destiny?

Why do people climb Mount Everest? Why do men and women push the barriers on speed, performance, and intellectual ability? Why do scientists study the origins of life on earth? Why do astronomers peer as far as technology will allow into the farthest reaches of the ever-expanding universe?

Innate in mankind is a curiosity and desire for light and truth. It is what compels us to search for meaning and purpose in the universe and inside ourselves.

So back to the questions, "How can a person know God exists? Why did Heavenly Father created me with all these yearnings to understand myself and fulfill my destiny?" My answer is that a person needs to open himself or herself to experience God and the life that Heavenly Father has created all around.

We need to delve deeply into the spiritual fabric of our mortal existence and *experience*, as designed by Heavenly Father. He is manifest in it, "and any man who hath seen any or the least of these hath seen God moving in his majesty and power" (D&C 88:47).

In other words, you can't kneel down in prayer one time, hurl a bunch of questions out into the cosmos, and expect the heavens to open and bestow answers. You need to meet Heavenly Father on His journey toward you.

It's an active and sometimes lengthy searching process. It's more than passively hoping Heavenly Father will reach out, tap you on the shoulder, and tell you He exists. Rather, He wants you to find Him in deep, personal, and meaningful ways. When people are searching for meaning and trying to understand the complexities of life, they are setting the stage to experience God.

Key to all of this is the realization that Heavenly Father is reaching out to you, just like the Armenian father who searched through the rubble for his son. This humble and dedicated Armenian father had made a promise to his son that he would always come looking for him. Heavenly Father has done the same for you through a covenant, and "there is nothing that the Lord thy God shall take in his heart to do but what he will do it" (Abraham 3:17).

In Your Search as an Honest Truth Seeker

Are you an honest truth seeker? Are you sincerely interested in truth? As you discover truth, will you accept it as part of your belief system in all its shades and hues—good and evil, beauty and ugliness, light and darkness? Or are you satisfied with becoming a law unto yourself and living in a world inside a mind of falsehoods and misdirected perceptions?

In your search as an honest truth seeker to find God, you must question everything about life and Heavenly Father, even the seeming contradictions of God. Start with the questions, "Is there a God? Who is He?" And then search diligently. The contents of this book were written with these questions in mind.

It is important to think and ponder seriously about who you are, why you exist, and how you came into existence. What is your purpose in life? Why are you here? What did you bring with you from a premortal existence? This was easy for Mozart. As a child, he would walk about town or through the woods and compose symphonies in his mind. Did he come here with that ability? What abilities did you bring with you? What abilities are you responsible for developing in your life? With those abilities, what responsibility do you have to bless the lives of others?

In your search, it is also important that you don't go running to people you may know in the Church or out of the Church, believers or disbelievers, and accept their views and opinions without judging for yourself. Don't look to the so-called experts, philosophers, other religions, family, or even the prophet. They may be helpful, but your quest for truth and learning about yourself and God is between you and Him. Strip everything away and don't be comfortable.

Also, suspend your disbelief and open yourself to receiving revelations and experiences from God. Set aside all your baggage and even possibly hard feelings for others. Then be honest with yourself if the things you are feeling are real and true. You will know. These experiences are deeper than a forced self-deception.

And, in your search as an honest truth seeker to find God, don't get lost in the philosophies of the world. However, I encourage you to learn what you can about the philosophies of men. Learn everything as the Lord intends us to do as we become more like Him. We should add to the philosophies of the world and men. The Lord knows all things, and we should to; in fact, He has commanded it. As members of the Church, we should join in the conversation and point to truth and have an honest open dialogue on all things with all peoples.

The Hard Work of Setting the Stage for Revelation

Alma, the father of Alma the Younger, knew of the hard work and heavy lifting needed to find and know God. He told his sons, "Behold, I have fasted and prayed many days that I might know these things of myself. And now I do know of myself that they are true." Alma broke through the rubble of his life, reaching up to know God, and a connection was made. Alma continued, "For the Lord God hath made them manifest unto me by his Holy Spirit; and this is the spirit of revelation which is in me" (Alma 5:46).

In our day, Harvard business professor Clayton Christensen had a similar struggle to Alma's. But through sacrifice, perseverance, and many late nights, he made the connection to a Heavenly Father reaching down to him.[30]

Clayton received a scholarship to Oxford University as a Rhodes scholar. As a recipient of the Rhodes Scholarship, he had multiple demands on his time, and additionally he intended to obtain a degree in applied econometrics—normally a three-year program—in just two years. At this same time, he began to question if the Book of Mormon was true.

Clayton had read the Book of Mormon seven times prior to this. After each reading of the book, he knelt in prayer and asked God if the book was true. He had received no answer. Reflecting on his past reading, he concluded, each time he had read it, that it was an assignment with the goal of simply finishing the book. As he commenced his studies at Oxford, he realized that he needed to know if the Book of Mormon was true. He felt a desperate desire to know for himself if it was true. (Was the need and desperation he felt from a loving Heavenly Father reaching through the rubble?)

Despite the demanding rigors of his academic program, Clayton decided to read the Book of Mormon every night of the week from eleven to midnight, this time with the purpose of determining if the book was true. He recollected wondering if he could afford to spend an entire hour each night, but he continued diligently. On the first night, he knelt in prayer by his little heater and prayed out loud, telling Heavenly Father he was desperate to know if the Book of Mormon was true. This real intent is a characteristic of a truth seeker.

Night after night, for that hour Clayton would read a page, stop at the end, and ponder what he read. He asked himself, *Could this have been written by a charlatan who was trying to deceive people, or was this really written by a prophet of God? And what does it mean for me in my life?* Then Clayton knelt in prayer and asked, "Please tell me if this is a true book." Then he would sit in the chair, pick up the book, and read another page.

Eventually, in the damp, cold room in Oxford, reading near the end of 2 Nephi, Clayton reported, "All of a sudden there came into that room a beautiful, warm, loving spirit that just surrounded me and permeated my soul, and enveloped me in a feeling of love that I just had not imagined I could feel. And I began to cry, and I didn't want to stop crying because as I looked through my tears at the words in the Book of Mormon, I could see truth in those words that I never imagined I could comprehend before. And I could see the glories of eternity and . . . what God had in store for me as one of His sons."[31]

Clayton reported that this spirit stayed with him for the whole hour, and then every evening as he prayed and sat with the Book of Mormon by the little heater in his room, that same spirit returned, and it changed his heart and his life forever.

The Book of Mormon prophet Enos had a wrestle before God, like the sincere truth seekers Alma and Clayton Christensen. The record of his backstory is sparse, but if he was wrestling, he had probably been searching for an extended period of time. Enos related, "I went to hunt beasts in the forests; and the words which I had often heard my father speak concerning eternal life, and the joy of the saints, sunk deep into my heart. And my soul hungered; and I kneeled down before my Maker, and I cried unto him in mighty prayer and supplication for mine own soul; and all the day long did I cry unto him; yea, and when the night came I did still raise my voice high that it reached the heavens" (Enos 1:4).

Again, here was someone who had been searching for a while and then prayed all "day long" and into the night. Persistence is another characteristic of a truth seeker.

Like Enos, as I seek to receive spiritual communication, I find it helpful to get out into the mountains or listen to beautifully composed music. It helps to be in a different frame of mind. I like to surround myself with the beauty and majesty of God's creations. It is my belief that the literal glory of God reflects off of snowy mountaintops or calm mountain lakes. As the Doctrine and Covenants teaches, "The elements are the tabernacle of God." (D&C 93:35). The glory of God is in and through the elements, even while he is an embodied Man of Holiness. Our brains are designed to perceive the things of this world based on the light that reflects off them.

As you move in the direction of God, He will manifest Himself to you in your moments of deep thought and reflection. But to get into that mindset takes real effort of body, mind, and soul. This is not a casual process. It takes time, pondering, and questioning. It mostly centers on deep and personal reflection on who you are—the mystery of your being. It takes work, mental and spiritual. Too often we expect God to do all the work. You must realize that He is constrained from reaching out to you in certain ways because of how He has structured reality. He must preserve the dimension of faith.

Past Spiritual Experiences

You have likely had spiritual experiences in the past, but the memory and light of those experiences may have dimmed and now you wonder if they ever really happened. In his "Letter to a Doubter" Dr. Terryl L. Givens, professor of literature and religion at the University of Richmond, wrote,

> At the same time, remembering rather than experiencing moves us toward greater independence, and insulates us from the vicissitudes of the moment. Brigham said God's intention was to make us as independent in our sphere, as he is in his. That is why the heavens close from time to time, to give us room for self-direction. That is why the Saints rejoiced in a Pentecostal day in Kirtland's temple, but were met with silence in Nauvoo. Silence—and their memories of Kirtland. One can see the Lord gently tutoring us to replace immediacy with memory, in section 6, when he says to Oliver, "If you desire a further witness, cast your mind upon the night that you cried unto me in your heart, that you might know concerning the truth of these things. Did I not speak peace to your mind concerning the matter? What greater witness can you have than from God?" . . . [Citing C. S. Lewis,] "God allows spiritual peaks to subside into (often extensive) troughs in order for 'servants to finally become Sons,' 'stand[ing] up on [their] own legs—to carry out from the will alone duties which have lost all relish . . . growing into the sort of creature He wants [them] to be.' "[32]

Dr. Givens also wrote, "Finally, find solace in what I have called the fellowship of the desolate. With Mother Teresa, who said, "I am told God lives in me and yet the reality of darkness and coldness and emptiness is so great that nothing touches my soul. . . . Heaven from every side is closed."[33]

Yes, God may seem distant to you. But from my experiences, I know He is there. All I can hope for is that you can come to know God in your own personal way. Keep searching, reading, pondering, praying, and doing whatever else it takes.

As you read through the remaining chapters in this book, please do so as an honest truth seeker who is searching for meaning in who you are and the mystery of your being.

Chapter 4
Pilate's Rhetorical Question: What Is Truth?

"To this end was I born, and for this cause came I into the world, that I should bear witness unto the truth. Every one that is of the truth heareth my voice. Pilate saith unto him, What is truth?" (John 18:37–38).

What is truth? How exactly does truth bring me freedom? What is honest truth-seeking?

Before sentencing Him to die on the cross, Pontius Pilate, the Roman prefect ruling the province Judea, ironically asked the Savior, "What is truth?"

Man is a truth-seeking, meaning-making intelligence. It seems, however, that some people are more earnest seekers than other people. Clement of Rome was such as a person.

From a family of wealth and means in the first century AD, Clement set out to travel the ancient world, his soul longing for meaning. Nothing else mattered to him. In the beginning of Clement's *Recognitions*, he stated that what prompted him to investigate the gospel of Christ was his desire to get answers to his questions about why he existed, where truth existed, and the what the meaning of life was. Specifically, he wanted to know, "When was this world made? What was there before it? Was it always there? Is there a life after death?"[34]

Clement had real intent, a hunger and thirst for truth and meaning.

Clement started his search for answers at the school he attended. He reported that no professor or philosopher could answer his questions satisfactorily. The teachers and rabbis did not like these questions from Clement or others. In fact, at a later date, the rabbis declared that "anyone who studies the subjects of the Creation . . . or who puts his mind to the questions: What is above? What is below? What is beyond? What is in the eternities? . . . It were better for him had he not come into the world."[35]

Next Clement sought out every notable teacher in Rome to no avail. This deepened the anxiety he felt about his existence. He worked tirelessly searching for answers, not able to eat or sleep. A friend counseled the young Clement to travel to Egypt and search through the mystery cults of the Egyptians. On the way to Egypt, Clement came across a Christian missionary named Barnabas, who advised Clement to travel to Caesarea to talk with the Apostle Peter. So Clement traveled to meet Peter in Jerusalem, where he converted to Christianity.

Hugh Nibley wrote the following about Clement's conversation with the Apostle Peter:

> Peter compares the world in which we live to a great house filled with dense smoke—blinding smoke produced by human unbelief, malice, ambition, greed, etc. Because of this smoke, the people who live in the house can see nothing clearly, but we must imagine them groping about with weak and running eyes, coughing and scolding, bumping into each other, tripping over furniture, trying to make out a bit of reality here and there—a corner, a step, a wall—and then trying to fit their desperate and faulty data together to make some kind of sense.[36]

Dr. Gertrude Specht

In our day, Dr. Gertrude Specht, another soul—searching for truth, seeking light and intelligence but not knowing where to find it—sat in her apartment in Munich, Germany. The following report is from a missionary who had become acquainted with her.

> A knock came at the door. She opened it and invited two Mormon missionaries inside her home. She seated the missionaries in her study and sat behind her desk. She showed the elders her three PhDs in theology, philosophy, and European history. Next she showed them a row of books she had written. Then she announced that she was a theology professor at the University of Munich.

"What would you like to discuss today?" she asked the elders. "The Book of Mormon," answered one of the missionaries.

The elders left Dr. Specht with a Book of Mormon. When they returned two months later they found the soon-to-be Sister Specht dressed in white at a baptismal service. The elder reported that Dr. Specht stood in front of this small congregation and said, "Before I'm baptized I'd like to tell you of my feelings. In Amos 8:11 it says there will be a famine in the work of God. I've been in that famine for seventy-six years. Why do you think I have three PhDs? I've been hungering for the truth and have been unable to find it. Then 8 ½ weeks ago, two boys walked into my home. I want you to know these boys are very nice and wonderful young men, but they didn't convert me. They couldn't; they don't know enough." And then she smiled and said, "But since the day they walked in my door I have read the Book of Mormon, the Doctrine and Covenants, the Pearl of Great Price, all of Talmage's great writings, *Evidence and Reconciliations* by John A. Widtsoe, and twenty-two other volumes of Church doctrine." She then said, "I don't think you members know what you have."

She continued, according to the elder, "After those years of studying philosophy, I picked up the Doctrine and Covenants and read a few little verses that answered some of the greatest questions of Aristotle and Socrates! When I read those verses, I wept for four hours." Then she said again, "I don't think you members know what you have. Don't you understand the world is in a famine? Don't you know we are starving for what you have? I am like a starving person being led to a feast. And over these 8 ½ weeks I have been able to feast in a way I have never known possible."[37]

To a cynic like me, it sounds almost too good to be true—that a religious scholar sat with two humble missionaries and recognized the truth that she had been searching for her entire life. Though she passed away in 1986, Gertrude Specht did join the church in Germany in the 1970s. The November 1973 *Church News* published an article reporting on a large gathering of European Saints. The articles stated of Sister Specht,

> As a young woman Gertrud Specht attended the University of Munich from which she obtained a doctorate degree in economics. Later, while doing historical research, she became interested in genealogical work and spent a great deal of time collecting information concerning her ancestors without knowing why it was so important. She has always

> had a burning desire to learn. She speaks six languages and is currently, at the age of 78, enrolled in philosophy classes at the university. Because a doctorate degree is so respected in German society, she has been able to open many doors to the Church since her baptism. She was set apart as a district missionary and has helped many people gain testimonies of the gospel. She always attends their baptisms.
>
> Sister Specht remarked that three years ago her life seemed all but over, but then came her conversion to the true church. She has been a member less than three years, having been baptized shortly before her 75th birthday. Now, she says, her life has "expanded to tremendous proportions."[38]

The restored gospel answered many philosophical and theological questions for Sister Spect. While we don't know exactly what questions she had, Heavenly Father has restored many thought-provoking teachings through the Prophet Joseph Smith. These teachings include:

The eternal nature of man's identity: Whereas the world believes that the soul of man was created at his mortal birth or is a product of evolutionary processes, Joseph Smith revealed that "the mind or the intelligence which man possesses is co-equal [co-eternal] with God himself."[39] This is also revealed in Doctrine and Covenants 93:29, which tells us that "man was also in the beginning with God. Intelligence, or the light of truth, was not created or made, neither indeed can be." Joseph also taught, "God himself, finding he was in the midst of spirits and glory, because he was more intelligent, saw proper to institute laws whereby the rest could have a privilege to advance like himself."[40] Joseph Smith further stated, "The relationship we have with God places us in a situation to advance in knowledge. He has power to institute laws to instruct the weaker intelligences, that they may be exalted with Himself, so that they might have one glory upon another, and all that knowledge, power, glory, and intelligence, which is requisite in order to save them in the world of spirits."[41]

The purpose of mortality: Heavenly Father's purpose in creating this earth, upon which we live to experience contradictions, die, and be resurrected, is to provide us with exposure to the good and evil that naturally exists in the universe that we inhabit with Him. It was our choice to come here to experience the opposition in all things that naturally exist so we could partake more fully of the type of life Heavenly

Father lives. As Joseph Smith explained, "All the minds and spirits that God ever sent into the world are susceptible of enlargement. . . . The relationship we have with God places us in a situation to advance in knowledge."[42]

The nature and character of Heavenly Father: Heavenly Father has within Himself all the powers of life, intelligence, truth, and glory. They are part of His being, as well as a product of His mind. He is all-powerful, the Creator of worlds without number. He is holy and just, filled with light, intelligence, and heart-felt compassion for us. Joseph Smith said of Heavenly Father, "[He] sittest enthroned, with glory, honor, power, majesty, might, dominion, truth, justice, judgment, mercy, and an infinity of fulness, from everlasting to everlasting" (D&C 109:77).

The nature and character of Christ: The glory and power of the Father dwell in Christ, and it is through Christ that man receives the powers of life and light as benevolent gifts from the Father. All things relating to life and eternal progress for us, past, present, and future, come from Christ, as dictated by the Father.

The premortal Christ: Christ acquired much of the Father's divine nature and glory prior to His time in mortality. To live as a mortal, Jesus suppressed His divine nature to experience all the woes of mortality, with all the contrasts of pain and pleasure—joy and sadness, *ad infinitum*—so He could fully relate to us as we experience this world through our fallen natures. In Gethsemane and in His daily walk, Christ descended below all things. Because of this, He knows the heights and the depths of existence, all to better understand us, culminating with the ultimate experience of bearing each of our sorrows in the Garden of Gethsemane.

The power of the Light of Christ: The Light of Christ is derived from the Father's glory, light, intelligence, and power. As these spiritual substances dwell in Christ, they are the source of the Light of Christ. Through the Father's divine nature, Jesus Christ is the Light and the Life of the World. "He that ascended up on high, as also he descended below all things, in that he comprehended all things, that he might be in all and through all things, the light of truth; which truth shineth. This is the light of Christ" (D&C 88:6–7).

The enabling powers of the Atonement: Through the Atonement, men and women who have come unto Christ are given spiritual powers in mortality to benefit from Christ's indwelling relationship with the Father, as His Only Begotten. This life is not only about being forgiven of sins we commit. We may receive of Christ's life-giving light to transform our fallen natures.

Conclusion

Poets, philosophers, theologians, and even prophets have been soul searchers for truth. Under the surface of day-to-day life, Heavenly Father is reaching out to you and all His children, inviting, encouraging, and loving you as an uncreated being to become who you are as your highest and most fulfilled self. He has been doing this since time immemorial.

President Brigham Young once remarked, "If we could see our Father who dwells in the heavens . . . he would be as familiar to us in the expression of his countenance, and we should be ready to embrace him and fall upon his neck and kiss him. . . . And there is no other one item that will so much astound you, when your eyes are opened in eternity."[43]

Chapter 5
An Intelligent Designer? Making the Case for Faith in God

"God used beautiful mathematics in creating the world."[44]

Is God hiding from me? Is the evidence of an intelligent designer enough to prove the existence of God?

A reporter of a national news broadcast started out his report as follows.[45]

> A mild afternoon in Lynchburg, Virginia. Eban and Holley Alexander are at a high school soccer game. . . . They are a perfectly ordinary American family with an extraordinary story. They have been touched with a medical miracle and maybe more.
>
> "It was impossible after impossible after impossible," said Dr. Eban Alexander.
>
> [The reporter introduced Dr. Alexander:] A Harvard-trained neurosurgeon, who was a skeptic when it came to religion, survived a near-death experience and now carries the memory of what he says is his journey to heaven, a journey that all of his scientific training cannot explain.
>
> On November 10, 2008, Dr. Alexander woke with a searing headache. When his wife, Holley, checked in on him, he was having a tremendous seizure. . . . He was rushed to the hospital, where he worked as a neurosurgeon, stricken with an extremely rare and virulent e coli meningitis infection that was ravaging his brain plunging him into a coma. In fact, doctors gave him no chance to live.

"Did you go to heaven?" the reporter asked Dr. Alexander.

"Yes. In every sense of the word that was what my experience showed me."

His first recollection he said was being a speck of pure awareness in a dark and murky underworld.

"Then I was rescued by this beautiful spinning white light that had a melody that was indescribably beautiful. It opened up into a bright valley—just an incredible, rich, ultra-real world of indescribable complexity."

[The reporter then said,] "God was there, he says, and he encountered him through an orb of brilliant light. He soared on the wing of a butterfly with a beautiful young woman as his companion. And the young women gave him a message to take back from heaven."

"'You are loved. You are cherished. There is nothing you have to fear. There is nothing you can do wrong,'" said Dr. Alexander, referring to the message he received.

"It's a beautiful vision, but of heaven? A lot of people are going to say, 'Doctor, it was a hallucination. Your brain got zapped by this disease, all the wires got crossed, and you saw a girl on a butterfly wing. You were spinning up in a melody."

Dr. Alexander responded, "I know this was not a hallucination, a dream, or what we call a confabulation. I know that it really occurred and I know that it occurred outside of my brain."

"But how can you even suggest that, much less explain that this experience is proof of heaven?"

Showing the reporter his brain scan, Dr. Alexander said, "It wasn't leaving any part of my cortex unaffected."

"So your conclusion is because the outer area of your brain, which is higher functioning, was covered with the infection, and what you experienced in the coma wasn't part of the brain."

Dr. Alexander confirmed the summation.

Many neuroscientists are deeply skeptical of Dr. Alexander's claims, arguing that his brain must have produced the vision somehow, most likely when he came out of coma. But something else happened.

After he was adopted, Dr. Alexander saw a picture of his sister from his biological family who died years ago—a women he never knew.

"I knew who my guardian angel was on the butterfly wing. It was the most profound experience I ever had in this life," said Dr. Alexander.

[The reporter questioned,] "Your sister by birth—from a family you did not know because you were adopted, who died several years ago, and who you had never met—you saw while you were in coma?"

Dr. Alexander responded, "Yes, and that was the key. That explained everything."

[The reporter ended his segment showing the Alexander family around the kitchen table praying over their evening meal.] Dinnertime at the Alexander home. They were not a particularly religious family before Eban's coma. He was a skeptic. Not anymore.

[Dr. Alexander ended the TV news segment by saying,] "This proves that our soul, our consciousness, our spirit doesn't depend on the existence of the brain and the body at all, and easily is freed up to a much higher state of knowing when it is freed from this body."

Reasonable Doubt, Reasonable Belief

Though Dr. Alexander said he has proof in the existence of God, in all due respect no one can prove or disprove definitively, beyond a shadow of a doubt, that God exists. All that you or I can do is show *reasonable* doubt or belief. In this life, we must walk by faith, as frustrating as that is for people searching for answers to the deeper questions about life.

Intelligent design is the belief that the universe was not created by chance but by an intelligent entity. When someone looks up into the vaulted starry skies or into the face of a newborn baby and sees order and purpose, that *evidence* can lead them to a belief in a divine creator, and by extension a belief in God.

As the Primary song goes, "Whenever I hear the song of a bird / Or look at the blue, blue sky, / Whenever I feel the rain on my face / Or the wind as it rushes by, / Whenever I touch a velvet rose / Or walk by our lilac tree, / I'm glad that I live in this beautiful world / Heav'nly Father created for me."[46]

When I sang those words as a child, it made sense that "Heav'nly Father created this beautiful world for me." Like most, as a child I had a fascination with nature, from the tiny insects burrowing in the dirt to the chirping and flight of the birds in the trees overhead. I experienced the joy of it all, with the warmth of the sun on my skin as I searched through the stream behind my house, another place of awe and wonder. In the evenings, my parents would take me to the beach, another marvelous ecosystem. Warm sand, frothy turbulent waves, and off in the distance the magnificent sun dipping below the horizon and bringing a cold chill of darkness. Soon, a silver moon lighted over the white crash of the waves.

As a young man, every summer my ward ventured out into the untraveled parts of Yosemite National Park. We crossed over Tioga Pass, the only entrance on the eastern side of the park. The mountain ascending to the pass was steep and rugged, with long stretches of granite and sparse pine trees that had somehow taken root in the cracks. There was a silent, isolated beauty to the country. Because it is accessible only by foot, few people traveled there. Reaching the summit, we peered over the mountaintop to witness the breathtaking scenery of Yosemite. We made our way down the other side of the mountain along the narrow trail and set up camp for the night by a small lake.

I was a few weeks shy of my twelfth birthday. In the coolness of the morning, I walked around the lake with the rising sunlight glinting off the water. I situated myself on a boulder and could see across a great portion of this untamed wilderness. I still remember the images looking out across the mountains, the granite cliffs, and the rocky overlooks in soft colors from the rising sun. A cold morning wind came across the lake carrying the pine and brush scents of the mountains. I felt the coolness of it on my face.

I remember ideas coming into my mind that Heavenly Father created this beautiful mountain scene to be enjoyed. In a spiritual way, in my eleven-year-old heart, I felt Heavenly Father created the entire world for His children to experience a life unique to them. I felt a burning in my bosom that Heavenly Father was real, that He cared about me, and that He was a man like my father. I think of the power of this experience even now, many years later.

Back to the point of this chapter, this was a truly wonderful spiritual experience that indicated to me that there is a God, but this experience also was not definitive proof of God's existence.

Setting the Stage for Revelation from God

Pius X declared that "by the natural light of reason, God can be certainly known and therefore His existence demonstrated through the things that are made, [that is to say] through the visible works of creation, as the cause is known through its effects."[47] To Korihor, an anti-Christ, the Book of Mormon prophet Alma stated, "The scriptures are laid before thee, yea, and all things denote there is a God; yea, even the earth, and all things that are upon the face of it, yea, and its motion, yea, and also all the planets which move in their regular form do witness that there is a Supreme Creator" (Alma 30:44).

Elder Douglas L. Callister taught, "With its 107 million cells, connected to the brain by over 1 million neurons, the eye is more perfect than any camera ever invented. It caused Charles Darwin [the father of evolutionary theories] to admit, "That the eye with all its inimitable contrivances . . . could have been formed by natural selection, seems, I freely confess, absurd in the highest sense."[48]

As impressive as that fact is about the development of the human eye over nine months of gestation from conception, it doesn't definitely prove God's existence. But for many people, these miraculous wonders do point us to God. Elder Callister continued, "The evidence of Heavenly Father's existence is everywhere: in every newborn babe and in every system, part, and parcel of the unending and orderly universe, including our own bodies. He is evidenced in every sunset, work of art, and passage of music, all of which He has provided to gladden the heart and bring beauty to our lives."[49]

As stated earlier, it is impossible to know definitively that God exists, but I believe that by surrounding us with so many marvels and wonders of nature and life, Heavenly Father is setting the stage for us to receive revelation of Him. When our thoughts drift to questions of how there could be so much design and order, we become more open to the idea of an omnipotent designer. And ultimately, revelation and personal experience with Heavenly Father are the only ways to know of God's existence.

Proving Man's Evolution

Of course, not everyone agrees that Heavenly Father created this beautiful world. For example, social anthropologist Robert Briffault said, "No myth of miraculous creation is so marvelous as the face of man's evolution."[50] Or as evolutionary biologist Richard Dawkins said, "You can't even begin to understand biology, you can't understand life, unless you understand what it's all there for, how it arose—and that means evolution."[51]

Yet, evolutionists face the same predicament of definitive proof that believers face. The Book of Mormon prophet Alma knew this. He challenged Korihor by asking, "And now what evidence have ye that there is no God, or that Christ cometh not? I say unto you that ye have none, save it be your word only" (Alma 30:40).

The watchmaker argument states that design implies a designer. This argument has been used to argue intelligent design and the existence of God since 1802, when William Paley published his book *Natural Theology*. But in 1859, a counterargument to Paley's book came when Charles Darwin published *The Origin of the Species*, which put forth his theory of natural selection as an explanation for the complexity and biological diversity of the natural world.

As the watchmaker analogy goes, you are walking along the beach and stumble upon a finely crafted pocket watch. Did the watch mysteriously spring into existence or did a watchmaker leave it there?

The watchmaker analogy consists of comparing natural phenomena to a watch. The complex inner workings of a watch necessitate an intelligent designer. And by extension, the complexity of life, the universe, or anything complex necessitates a designer, and that designer is assumed to be God by many people.

When Darwin completed his studies of theology at Christ's College in 1831, he read Paley's *Natural Theology* and believed that the work gave rational proof of the existence of God. This was for the very reason that other people believed the watchmaker analogy—that living beings and things showed complexity and therefore were designed that way. However, on the voyage of *The Beagle*, Darwin found that nature was not so kindly ordered, and the array of species did not support ideas of divine creation as the world understood them at that time in history. In 1838, shortly after his return, Darwin conceived his theory, which stated that natural selection, not divine design, was the best explanation for gradual change in populations over many generations. Darwin wrote in his autobiography,

> Though I did not think much about the existence of a personal God until a considerably later period of my life, I will here give the vague conclusions to which I have been driven. The old argument of design in nature, as given by Paley, which formerly seemed to me so conclusive, fails, now that the law of natural selection has been discovered. We can no longer argue that, for instance, the beautiful hinge of a bivalve shell must have been made by an intelligent being, like the hinge of a door by man. There seems to be no more design in the variability of organic beings and in

> the action of natural selection, than in the course which the wind blows. Everything in nature is the result of fixed laws.[52]

There is evidence of design in nature, but in our day evolutionary biologists point to evidence of frustration of design and slow developments. They point to fossil remains of entire species now extinct. Evolutionists argue that evolution is purposive. New life forms originate from higher forms and adapt from environment to environment. In short, evolutionists demonstrate there is struggle in nature as there is in all life on this planet "an opposition in all things" (2 Nephi 2:11), as the prophet Lehi pointed out.[53]

Darwin predicted that over time, with further excavations, fossil records would prove him correct and it would show slow but gradual change or mutations from one species to another. However, 150 years later, we have enough fossil records to contradict Darwin, but not entirely. Evolutionary biologist and Harvard professor Stephen Gould in 1972 proposed evidence contrary to the theory of slow, gradual mutations. In what he called "punctuated equilibrium," Gould reported the fossil record shows long periods of evolutionary stability, punctuated by rare instances of branching evolution or creative periods. These bursts of organic activity and development occur relatively rapidly. According to Gould, punctuated equilibrium revised a key pillar "in the central logic of Darwinian theory."[54]

I am not here to take down or disprove evolution (in fact, many things—after examining the evidence—I wholeheartedly believe). My point is that we do not have all the answers on creation and should continue researching and theorizing. An honest truth seeker cannot summarily dismiss the existence of God by our current knowledge base and evolutionary theories. Man does not have all the answers. Heavenly Father puts us on earth with a wonderful puzzle to solve, and we learn and grow as we work on it. Yet, there will come a day when all things will be revealed. As we read in Doctrine and Covenants 101:32–34, "In that day when the Lord shall come, he shall reveal all things—things which have passed, and hidden things which no man knew, things of the earth, by which it was made, and the purpose and the end thereof—things most precious, things that are above, and things that are beneath, things that are in the earth, and upon the earth, and in heaven."

What a day that will be!

Black Swans Exist after All

It is a logical paradigm that one cannot claim something does not exist. For example, if I had an object and told you to look for it, you cannot simultaneously look everywhere for that object. So if you looked in one corner of the vast universe and did not find God there, He may just be in another corner.

For almost all of human history, no one had ever seen a black swan. Juvenal, a Roman poet from the second century, wrote (translated from Latin), "A perfect wife is a rare bird; a rare bird in the earth and most similar to a black swan." Fourteen centuries later, a common expression in sixteenth century England was "like finding a black swan" (as a statement of impossibility). The presumption the world over was all swans were white. No black swans had ever been seen and therefore were thought to not exist. But in 1697 in western Australia, a Dutch explorer discovered black swans. That belief once thought an impossibility became a known fact. So you can't say definitively that something does not exist, because one day you might find it.

Greater Questions?

Some of the greatest questions are *Where is God? Who is He?*, and *Why did He create you and me with all these yearnings to understand for ourselves?* A perfect and loving God would surely provide the means to find Him. So where does a truth seeker turn for definitive answers on God's existence? A member of the Church might quickly answer with things like the scriptures, spiritual experiences, the temple, prophets, modern-day revelation, and so on. A non-believer on the other hand might argue against these things, asking for visible, tangible, empirical proof.

It has been my experience that only through reason and revelation can we know of God. For me, the more diligently I seek after Him and answers about Him, the more I learn of Him. As I search in earnest, He gives me a little here and a little there, with things growing brighter and brighter. He gives me something and then waits on me to comprehend the revelation of additional truth to see what I will do with it. Then He gives me a little more. Sometimes it takes months or even years to receive the next big spiritual experience. In that time, the trial of faith stretches me. But I move on, living on the light I have received and doing my best to keep the commandments with full purpose of heart until the next ray of revelation shines in on my life.

However, an unbeliever might say that my pretended revelation is just self-fulfilling prophecy, that I have a lot at stake in supporting my belief system. It might be said that I am deceiving myself, that my mind is creating psychological experiences so I have justification to go on believing in God because it supports my worldview and gives me comfort. Maybe that's true. But there is no question more important than whether God exists, so it deserves serious pondering and attention.

Again, I suggest that it is only through reason and revelation, as our Heavenly Father intends, that we can know of Him and about Him. It all comes down to how diligently we seek after Him to experience Him.

Chapter 6
Making the Case for the Existence of God

"God is the tangential point between zero and infinity."[55]

How can I find and experience God? What evidence from the world around me proves or points to God? Or is He an absent Father, leaving me to my own devices in life?

Speaking of finding and experiencing God, Joan of Arc claimed that God reached out to her through the rubble of destruction of the Hundred Years' War. Joan of Arc was born to a peasant family and lived in northeast France from 1412–31. At fourteen, under what she claimed was divine guidance, she led the French army to several victories against England. At age nineteen, the English burned her at the stake for heresy.[56]

Joan of Arc claimed that three voices guided her in freeing her country from occupation, including Michael the Archangel, Saint Catherine of Alexandria, and Saint Margaret. She wrote,

> When I was thirteen, I had a voice from God to help me to govern myself. The first time, I was terrified. The voice came to me about noon: it was summer, and I was in my father's garden. . . . I saw it many times before I knew it was Saint Michael. . . . He was not alone, but duly attended by heavenly angels. . . . He told me Saint Catherine and Saint Margaret would come to me, and I must follow their counsel; that they were appointed to guide and counsel me in what I had to do, and that I must believe what they would tell me, for it was at our Lord's command.[57]

Making the Case for the Existence of God

Few believers in God have actually seen Him for themselves. For many, the beauty, wonder, and design of nature and life are enough to tip the scale. From there, people begin to see God's handiwork woven into the fabric of our existence, psychologies, and natures. In this great debate over God's existence, the side we choose influences how we perceive the purpose of life and our identities as sons and daughters of a loving, holy, infinite Father or as descendants hearkening back to before the origin of man.

In the spirit of truth-seeking, openness, and fairness, it is instructive to review both sides of the arguments for and against the existence of God. This chapter is a review of the arguments for God's existence, employed by theologians and philosophers through the history of man. Not all of these ideas provide conclusive evidence of the existence or nonexistence of God, and each has its strengths and weaknesses. In the following chapter, we will review arguments against God's existence used throughout the centuries.

The Majority, Sheer Number of Witnesses, and Christological Arguments

The majority argument holds that the belief in God by the majority of people through recorded history provides *prima facie* evidence of God's existence, whether a group of people believes in a single supreme being or multiple deities.

The sheer number of witnesses argument is that there is empirical evidence that God has revealed Himself to individuals and groups of people, and these events have been recorded as historical events. An example of this is in the Bible: the Savior's (as the God of the Old Testament) involvement with the Hebrews. Similarly, another example is the appearance of Heavenly Father, Jesus Christ, and angels to Joseph Smith and others, subsequent to and following the translation of the Book of Mormon.

The Christological argument holds that, based on historical records of many people who interacted with the resurrected Christ (after His death), He is the Son of God and thereby evidence of God. As we read in 3 Nephi, "And it came to pass that the multitude went forth, and thrust their hands into his side, and did feel the prints of the nails in his hands and in his feet" (3 Nephi 11:15). In the New Testament, many instances are recorded of Christ meeting with His Apostles after His Resurrection, even appearing to as many five hundred disciples at one time.

Those who refute these arguments often ask things like, "What if the people claiming divine authority are actually under psychological stress or mental delusions? Is this the cause for their belief that they are prophets, or even God or Christ?" Perhaps through hallucination or power of belief they are convinced that God has delivered a special message to them or that they are gods themselves. Then weak-minded and fanatical people ignore evidence around them because they desperately want to believe so they can belong to the movement.

Regarding the majority argument, why are there billions upon billions of people who have lived on earth who God has not revealed Himself to directly or through His prophets? Why only a select, chosen few?

Testimony and Miracles

The power of testimony argument is closely related to the power of the witnesses argument. Philosopher of religion Richard Swinburne argued that it is a "principle of rationality" that a person should accept the testimony of others' experiences with God unless there are strong reasons for not doing so, such as motive or deception.[58]

Along these same lines, the witness of miracles argument states that you can believe the testimonies of people who recorded supernatural events to establish the existence of God. Based on the credibility of the witnesses, you can believe these witnesses who record miraculous healings, divine interventions, or open visions, especially if no physical cause can be identified that produced said effect. The Book of Mormon prophet Mormon questioned, "Has the day of miracles ceased?" (Moroni 7:35).

And regarding testimony, philosopher Jean-Jacques Rousseau, in his work *Émile*, spoke to the dynamics of inner religious experience. In what Rousseau called *impulses of our hearts*, he asserted that when a person ponders God's existence, they encounter nothing but contradictions. Rousseau claimed that the impulses of our hearts are of more value than the concrete cognitive understanding of God. These impulses proclaim "clearly to us the truths of natural religion, namely, the existence of God and the immortality of the soul"[59] and include the impulses of our hearts when we marvel at a newborn infant being cradled in her mother's arms, the heart-pounding beauty of a symphony, or the feelings of love that vibrate through a mother as she watches her child's carefree play under a sycamore tree in blossom on a sunlit spring day.

A skeptic might argue that it is not rational or logical to follow the *impulses of our hearts* of emotions and feelings and set aside our precepts of concrete thinking. These emotional impulses should be checked against concrete ideas and philosophies, examining all available external evidence and societal norms.

John Locke, in his essay *Concerning Human Understanding*, insisted that everyone can know there is a divine Creator. He posited that each person "knows that he exists." As Descartes understood, *cogito ergo sum* ("I think, therefore I am"), Locke said, besides knowing he or she exists, furthermore each person knows that he or she (individually) is something. Everyone also knows that "a something" could not be produced by "a nothing." Therefore, whatever force brought man and all of nature into being also had to be "a something." Locke reasoned that it follows that "this something" must be superior to everything "this something" created and be the ultimate "good."

Locke added that through this line of reasoning, people could know many things about God. "This something" or Creator must be a reasoning and intelligent being to produce something as capable as man. Locke also reasoned that this Creator must also possess "a sense of compassion and love," as He instilled these qualities in man, along with a sense of right and wrong, justice, and "remorse for wrong." Locke further reasoned that the Creator must also be a great artist on the visual plane.

A critic of Locke could argue that this is only a psychological exercise in which we invent constructs in our minds based on preconceived beliefs. Starting with Locke's first question about knowing a person exists, there is a solipsistic philosophy movement that holds that anything outside one's own mind is unsure. The external world we think we are experiencing might not exist outside our minds.

Additionally, other arguments for the existence of God include the cosmological argument, which states that logically for the universe to exist, teaming with stars and planets, there had to be a first cause or prime mover, identified as God. As stated earlier about intelligent design, the teleological argument holds that universe's complexity and order are best explained by a Creator, and that because of the fact that only goals, purpose, and direction can occur in intelligent consciousness, God is the Creator of the universe. The ontological argument promoted by St. Anselm of Canterbury and others states that a Creator of the universe must exist "being greater than which cannot be conceived."[60] Simply put, if it is logically possible for God (a necessary being) to exist, then He exists.

Closely related is the anthropic argument, which suggests that man's existence is best explained by the existence of God. The moral argument says that man's perception of objective morality and ethics depends on the existence of God. And the transcendent argument puts forth that logic, science, and the mysteries of existence only make sense with God.

Even though these arguments point to God's existence, they are not definitive proof. Only by revelatorily experiencing God—which will be discussed later—can you know Him.

Chapter 7
Making the Case against God's Existence

"A man can no more diminish God's glory by refusing to worship Him than a lunatic can put out the sun by scribbling the word 'darkness' on the walls of his cell."[61]

If religious ideas are inconsistent or antiquated, does that disprove God? How can God, being all good, be responsible for a world with so much evil and suffering? Why would God create a world filled with paradoxes and contradictions of Him?

One test of life is whether we will be true to the power of our convictions. Even at peril and risk to ourselves, will we stand true to our beliefs?

Some people just won't be silenced regardless of the consequences, whether that means imprisonment in a dank prison cell in the fifteenth century or watching as flames ignite at your feet when you are tied to the stake for heresy. Thankfully, if you were to deny the existence of God today or publish ideas contrary to accepted Christian beliefs the consequences are not so dire at least in Western society.

But that wasn't always the case. At barely twenty years old, Michael Servetus published a work denouncing the prevailing beliefs of Christianity of his day.[62] Born in Spain in 1509, Servetus was trained by Dominicans at the University of Saragossa where he studied the Bible. In 1531, Servetus published *Errors of the Trinity*. He labeled those who believed in the Trinity as Tritheists (believers in three gods) or atheists.

Needless to say, the religious leaders of the day found the work blasphemous. The emperor even banned the book. To escape persecution, Servetus fled to France.

Naturally argumentative and contentious, Servetus wrote to the leading scholar, John Calvin, a proponent of the Trinity, asking what it meant for Jesus to be the Son of God and how man was to be born again. Servetus criticized Calvin's replies. He believed so strongly that he was right, he labeled Calvin and the pope as anti-Christs. This infuriated Calvin and needless to say the pope.

Desiring to restore Christianity to what he believed to be its original state of purity, in 1553, Servetus anonymously published *The Restitution of Christianity*. In his book, he continued to deny the Trinity and the incarnation of Christ, which were capital offenses. Contrary to the teachings of the reformers, Servetus also taught that both faith and works were necessary for salvation.

As a poke in the eye, Servetus secretly sent John Calvin a copy of his anonymous work. However, Roman Catholic authorities discovered Servetus's identity and arrested him on charges of blasphemy and heresy. He escaped and fled to Naples. On his way, he stopped at a church where Calvin was preaching. He was recognized and arrested again and eventually tried for heresy. At his trial, Servetus stunned the religious leaders with his belief that everything emanated from God, even the devil. He declared infant baptism an error.

The Geneva Council, supported by churches, condemned Servetus for heresy. Though Calvin insisted Servetus die, he urged that, in mercy, Servetus be executed by the sword, not by burning. But the Council rejected the suggestion. Calvin spent hours with Servetus, trying to turn him to the commonly accepted Christian doctrine, but Servetus stood fast. On October 27, 1553, Michael Servetus was burned at the stake for blasphemy and heresy. In the flames, he called on Jesus for mercy.

Heroically, he preferred to let someone take his life than consent to the conventional and commonly accepted point of view. Throughout history, many people have wavered and caved to the pressure. Knowing the stress of their situations, I do not judge them. But martyrs like Michael Servetus exemplify the importance of thinking critically about the existence of God and staying true to one's convictions.

Throughout the centuries, just as much thought and vigor has gone into arguing God out of existence as proving that He exists. This usually involves presenting religious ideas about Him as inconsistent, contradictory, or at odds with known scientific or historical facts. Therefore, insufficient reasons exist to believe.

The omnipotence paradox suggests that an omnipotent entity is logically contradictory. "Can God create a rock so big that He cannot lift it?" Or, "If God is all powerful, could God create a being more powerful than Himself?" The free will argument contests the existence of an omniscient God where His creatures (you and I) have free will; it argues that the two properties (an *omniscient* God and *free* creatures) are contradictory. According to the argument, if God already knows the future, then humanity is destined to corroborate with His knowledge of the future and does not have true free will to deviate from God's knowledge. Therefore, free will contradicts an omniscient God.

In the spirit of fairness and objectivity, let's review other arguments used by many to deny the existence of God. It is my personal opinion that testimonies and belief can be strengthened by exploring these arguments with facts and revealed latter-day truths.

The Theodicies

The most powerful and often-used argument for not believing in God is the apparent contradiction of the theodicies. *Theodicy* was coined in 1710 by German philosopher Gottfried Leibniz in his work *Théodicée*. This branch of theology attempts to defend the alleged attributes of God being omnipotent (all-powerful), omniscient (all-knowing), and omnibenevolent (all-good), in their absolute forms, with the moral and physical evil that naturally exists in the world and results in human suffering and misery.

For example, we hear Heavenly Father is omnipotent, omniscient, and omnipresent. Is Heavenly Father completely all-knowing, all-powerful, and all-present among His vast creations? If Heavenly Father is all-powerful and all-good, how can He allow evil and suffering to exist in the world He created?

This is an insolvable contradiction. Great thinkers have attempted to solve this paradox in a number of ways. They have said that evil and suffering from human perspective are not the same as from Heavenly Father's eternal perspective. Others have argued that Heavenly Father allows evil to exist so men will suffer and turn to Him.

To solve the contradiction of how an all-good God could create a world with evil and suffering, we need the revelations given to the Prophet Joseph Smith. Through modern revelation, we learn that we co-inhabit the universe with Heavenly Father. This universe is one that Heavenly Father did not create, but within the universe and according to His mastery of it He organizes worlds. He provides His children with premortal, mortal, and postmortal experiences that lead to redemption, resurrection, and eternal progress for His children *ad infinitum*. He is all-powerful in bringing to pass the immortality and eternal life of His children.

For example, given the nature of the universe we inhabit with Him, Heavenly Father did not create our world or any of His creations *ex nihilo* (out of nothing) simply because He willed our world to be created. Rather, Heavenly Father organized this earth and His vast creations from existing matter, according to eternal laws. He works with the structure and nature of the universe.

Additionally, because it is a necessary part of His plan, Heavenly Father must give His children their moral agency and free will. As a result, evil actions and resultant consequences may afflict His children. Elder Quentin L. Cook taught, "[To] those who do not have knowledge, understanding, or faith in the Father's plan—who look at the world only through the lens of mortality with its wars, violence, disease, and evil—this life can seem depressing, chaotic, unfair, and meaningless."[63] Yes, as one looks around the world, at the strong oppressing the weak or the rich grinding the faces of the poor, this can cause many people to wonder how an all-good, loving God could create such a world.

Here is where premortal perspective and context matter. Mankind's freedom is at the foundational core of its eternal existence—before mortality, during mortality, and eternally after mortality. We read in Doctrine and Covenants 93:30: "All truth is independent in that sphere in which God has placed it, to act for itself . . . otherwise there is no existence."

In other words, Heavenly Father is required in our mortal context to give us agency. We are agents unto ourselves, learning to stand independent in eternity by learning to be more like the Father and Son. With this understanding, Doctrine and Covenants 29:39 states, "And it must needs be that the devil should tempt the children of men, or they could not be agents unto themselves; for if they never should have bitter they could not know the sweet." Eternal life is God's life, and it is incomprehensibly sweet.

Continuing Elder Cook's statement from before, "Those without knowledge of the Father's plan do not understand what happened in the first act, or the premortal existence, and the purposes established there; nor do they understand the clarification and resolution that come in the third act, which is the glorious fulfillment of the Father's plan."[64]

An anonymous story of an exchange between a university professor and student is illustrative of the allegation about God being responsible for evil. The professor asked his class, "Did God create everything that exists?" A student said, "Yes, He did." "God created everything?" the professor asked. "Yes, sir," the student said. The professor then said, "If God created everything, then God created evil because evil exists, and according to the principle that our works define who we are, then God is evil." The student went quiet.

The professor was quite pleased with himself and boasted to the students that he had proven once more that the Christian faith is a myth. Another student raised his hand and said, "Can I ask you a question?" "Of course," replied the professor. The student stood and asked, "Professor, does cold exist?" "What kind of question is this? Of course it exists. Have you never been cold?" The students snickered at the young man's question.

The young man continued, "In fact, sir, cold does not exist. According to the laws of physics, what we consider cold is, in reality, the absence of heat. Every body or object is susceptible to study when it has or transmits energy, and heat is what makes a body or matter have or transmit energy. Absolute zero (negative 460 degrees Fahrenheit) is the total absence of heat; all matter becomes inert and incapable of reaction at that temperature. Cold does not exist. We have created this word to describe how we feel if we are lacking heat."

The student then asked, "Professor, does darkness exist?" The professor responded, "Of course it does."

The student replied, "Once again, you are wrong, sir. Darkness does not exist either. Darkness is just the absence of light. Light we can study, but not darkness. In fact, we can use Newton's prism to break white light into many colors and study the various wavelengths of each color. You cannot measure darkness. A simple ray of light can break into a world of darkness and illuminate it. How can you know how dark a certain space is? You measure the amount of light present. Isn't this correct? Darkness is a term used by people to describe what happens when there is no light present."

Finally, the young man asked the professor, "Sir, does evil exist?" Now uncertain, the professor responded, "Of course, as I have already said. We see it every day. It is in the daily example of man's inhumanity to others. It is in the multitude of crimes and violence everywhere in the world. These manifestations are nothing else but evil."

To this, the student replied, "Evil does not exist, sir, or at least it does not exist unto itself. Evil is simply the absence of God. It is just like darkness and cold—a word that people have created to describe the absence of God. God did not create evil. Evil is not like faith or love, which exist just as does light and heat. Evil is the result of what happens when humans do not have God's love present in their hearts. It's like the cold that comes when there is no heat or the darkness that comes when there is no light."

Inconsistencies in the Scriptures

One argument to refute the divine nature of scripture—the records of God's dealings with humanity—is their inconsistencies. It is a fact that contradictions and inaccuracies exist in the Bible. For example, in Acts 9:7, we read of Paul's vision of Christ: "And the men which journeyed with him stood speechless, hearing a voice, but seeing no man." But in Acts 22:9, "And they that were with me saw indeed the light, and were afraid; but they heard not the voice of him that spake to me."

What color was the robe placed on Jesus during His trial? In Matthew 27:28, we read the robe was scarlet. In John 19:2, it is recorded as purple. On the cross, what did the Roman soldiers give Christ to drink? Matthew 27:34 says vinegar. Mark 15:23 says it was wine with myrrh. Many other inconsistencies exist through scripture, mostly in the Old and New Testaments.

To be effective, the inconsistency argument requires that a person believes scriptural records are inerrant. Is the Bible inaccurate to the point that it has no credibility as a historical record of God's works? Or is there enough in the sum and substance of the Bible, written and translated over thousands of years, to make it credible as a record that builds faith?

The LDS answer to this criticism comes from Nephi. After hearing about his father's vision of the tree of life, Nephi desired to go to the Lord to understand the meaning of the vision. Nephi learned many things about the destiny of mankind. He learned that when the ancient biblical prophets wrote their records, they did so "in purity" (1 Nephi 13:25). Over time, their revelations, the "plain and most precious . . . covenants of the Lord" (verse 26), were taken away.[65] Nephi witnessed that these changes to the words of prophets would cause "an exceedingly great many do stumble," and Satan would gain "great power" (verse 29). In his final words, Mormon told us that the Book of Mormon was "written for the intent that ye may believe" the Bible (Mormon 7:9).

Destiny of the Unevangelized

The destiny of the unevangelized argument claims that God is capricious in determining the eternal destiny of His children. This unfairness in His nature is not consistent with His other attributes of goodness and justice claimed in the scriptures. Yes, some Christian theologians have taught that by God's whim some of His children are assigned to heaven and others to hell, where they suffer torment. The *unevangelized* are any born into situations where they would not have the opportunity to learn of God and know His requirements to gain an eternal reward.

Theologian John Calvin summarized his own views this way: "God preordained, for his own glory and the display of His attributes of mercy and justice, a part of the human race, without any merit of their own, to eternal salvation, and another part, in just punishment of their sin, to eternal damnation."[66] The Mormon answer to this argument is that God will save all His children in a kingdom of glory, except sons of perdition. Modern-day revelation is emphatic that, given their eternal agency and based on the type of law a person is willing to live, "Ye who are quickened by a portion of the celestial glory shall then receive of the same, even a fulness. And they who are quickened by a portion of the terrestrial glory shall then receive of the same, even a fulness. And also they who are quickened by a portion of the telestial glory shall then receive of the same, even a fulness . . . to enjoy that which they are willing to receive" (D&C 88:29–32).

Referring to the opportunities of eternal salvation and exaltation offered through temple work, President Wilford Woodruff remarked that he believed "few, if any, of the ancestors of the Latter-day Saints in the spirit world would choose to reject the message of salvation when they heard it."[67]

The Problem of Eternal Hell and the Argument from Nonbelief

The problem of eternal hell is the idea that eternal damnation for the actions committed in a finite existence of mortal life contradicts God's goodness. The LDS answer to this is that "it is not written that there shall be no end to this torment, but it is written endless torment . . . wherefore it is more express than other scriptures, that it might work upon the hearts of the children of men, altogether for my name's glory" (D&C 19:6–7).

Elder James E. Talmage stated, "To hell there is an exit as well as an entrance. Hell is no place to which a vindictive judge sends prisoners to suffer and to be punished principally for his glory; but it is a place prepared for the teaching, the disciplining of those who failed to learn here upon the earth what they should have learned. . . . When he reaches that stage the prison doors will open and there will be rejoicing among the hosts who welcome him into a better state."[68]

Taking into consideration the masses of humanity unaware of God's existence, the argument from nonbelief contests the existence of an all-powerful God who desires that humans believe in Him but does not do a better job of gathering believers. One dimension of the Mormon answer is that life is a test of morality for all people. Does a person need to know God through a religious institution while they are living to "prove" their compassion, integrity, selflessness, or other Christlike attributes? The great work of redemption of the dead is for this very purpose and was part of the gospel plan, as we read in the Doctrine and Covenants 124:33: "The same was instituted from before the foundation of the world."

Another dimension of the LDS answer is that all daughters and sons of God are under the watchful His eye and are placed on earth to further His work of salvation and exaltation of His children. In Maurice Maeterlinck's play *The Blue Bird*, unborn children are summoned to earth life as they stand perched atop a platform, peering down at the earth. The children wait for "Time" to call out their names as the moment of their descent arrives. The children look down upon the earth—some excited, others frightened, a few not wanting to be born at all. A beautiful melody rises to the platform. "Light" tells the children that they are hearing the "song of the mothers" calling to meet them.[69]

As one group approached the earth, the voices of the earthbound children were heard in the distance: "The earth! I can see it! How beautiful it is!" Then following these cries of joy (similar to morning stars shouting for joy; see Job 38:7), there issued forth a sweet song of expectancy and love. Maeterlinck wrote that it was the song of the mothers. Lilting melodies rose into the blueness of the sky from all parts of the earth. Each little spirit child was attracted to the spiritual and mortal parentage for which it had prepared itself.[70]

In the wisdom of Heavenly Father, not all of His children need to be Christian or seated on church pews, singing "Amazing Grace" to fulfill their assignments. Perhaps it was Feng-Shan Ho's premortal assignment and destiny to be a Chinese diplomat in Vienna to save two thousand Jews during World War II. Acting against orders of his superior, Ho, for humanitarian reasons, issued Jews visas to Shanghai.[71] He continued to issue these visas until he was ordered to return to China in May 1940. Or perhaps it was Paul Rusesabagina's premortal assignment and destiny to be a Rwandan hotel manager at a specific time and location where he would jeopardize his own life and that of his family as he hid and protected 1,268 Hutu and Tutsi refugees from being slaughtered by the Interahamwe militia during the Rwandan Genocide.[72]

Dr. Carlfred Broderick in his book *One Flesh, One Heart* described a woman he was counseling who suffered from recurrent bouts with anxiety and depression. He wrote,

> We got into her background and discovered that she had been raised by an abusive, alcoholic father and a neurotically sick mother who stayed in bed all the time and let her little girl do all of the cooking and cleaning. She confessed that she was still full of rage at her parents for so badly abusing her and full of envy for others who had experienced a normal, loving family relationship. She said that on several occasions when she had seen little girls being hugged and kissed by their loving fathers in Church she had to get up and leave.
>
> "The Lord knew what he was doing," she confessed, "when he sent me only boys to raise. Girls would have been too hard." Then she turned to me and said, "Where is the justice? How can God pretend to be just and send some little girls into homes where they are loved and petted and made to feel like somebody and others into homes where they are beat and molested and abused and neglected? What did I do in the pre-earth life to deserve such a family?"
>
> I felt inspired at that time to tell her that she had volunteered in the preexistence to be a savior on Mount Zion, to come to a family drowning in sickness and sin and to be the means of purifying that lineage. Before her in that line were generations of ugly, destructive, family relationships.
>
> Downstream from her purifying influence every generation would be blessed with light and love. The role of a savior, I said, is to suffer innocently for the sins of others that still others may not suffer. There can be no higher calling. She knew by the Spirit that what I suggested was true. That perspective gave her the strength to get on with her life. The last time I heard from her she had also exercised her prerogative to purify her line backward through temple work and was working hard on bringing her parents to see the light.[73]

Like many others, this woman became a transformational influence to stop a cycle of abuse and misery that existed generations before.

A third dimension and insight from modern-day revelation is that in His mercy, Heavenly Father does not give *all* commandments to all men and women so they are not accountable in a full measure to divine law. It is for this reason that He does not guide everyone into a Christian church or institution. The Apostle Paul taught that we commit sin only if, knowing the law, we disobey it. The Book of Mormon prophet Jacob testified that "where there is no law given . . . there is no condemnation," and that "the atonement satisfieth the demands of his justice upon all those who have not the law given to them" (2 Nephi 9:25–26).

Argument from Poor Design

Finally, the argument from poor design suggests that if God were all-powerful, He would have created a better humanity, with less physical failings and natures that are full of love and benevolence. This argument melts away when we understand God's purposes in our natures in mortality, and that God did not create us out of nothing but rather followed eternal law.

Church doctrine teaches that in our initial creation, Heavenly Father reached out to our individual intelligences—the light and truth of our being—through persuasion and love. The Father did all He could, waiting for us to respond, and then through spirit birth forged and infused into us all of His divinity that we were willing to accept. Joseph Smith stated, "The relationship we have with God places us in a situation to advance in knowledge. He has power to institute laws to instruct the weaker intelligences, that they may be exalted with Himself, so that they might have one glory upon another, and all that knowledge, power, glory, and intelligence, which is requisite in order to save them in the world of spirits."[74]

Heavenly Father's purpose in creating this earth—upon which we live as fallen beings, experience contradictions, and die and are resurrected to a higher state of glory—is to provide us exposure to the good and evil that naturally exists in the universe that we co-inhabit with Him. It was our choice to come here to experience the opposition in all things that naturally exist so we could partake more fully of the type of life Heavenly Father lives. "All the minds and spirits that God ever sent into the world are susceptible of enlargement and improvement. The relationship we have with God places us in a situation to advance in knowledge."[75]

The question of the poor design of the human body and human nature falls away when we look at a resurrected personage. President

Brigham Young taught, "Every man and woman that reaches to this unspeakable attainment will be as beautiful as the angels that surround the throne of God. . . . And, as we have borne the image of the earthly, we shall also bear the image of the heavenly."[76] Joseph Smith said of Moroni, "His whole person was glorious beyond description, and his countenance truly like lightning" (Joseph Smith—History 1:32). That is our future beyond this life.

Conclusion: Faith, Reason, and Seeking

So how do we search out and experience Heavenly Father? Is it even possible to know God as fallen mortals? How do we definitely know that God exists and why He created us with all these yearnings to understand ourselves and fulfill our destinies? Believers and nonbelievers alike face the same predicament. We only have fragmentary evidence at best. No absolute proof can be presented that God exists or doesn't exist. You cannot prove or disprove Him.

From chapter one, God was searching out C. S. Lewis in his conversion process, similar to the Armenia father. He does the same for you. He is tirelessly removing the rubble in your life, waiting anxiously for you to respond to Him. After all, it is "His work and glory to bring to pass the immortality and eternal life of man" (Moses 1:39).

C. S. Lewis commented that he was "feeling the unrelenting approach of him who I so earnestly desired not to meet."[77] He described the process as if it was being thrust upon him. He fought against it intellectually. He said of his conversion, "It came up from behind and took over my heart."[78] He could sense that something was happening to him and that he was caught up in the flow of the experience.

Again, we need to reject the simple premise that we must simply know God exists. What He desires most is that we have a relationship with Him and experience Him in His full glory, light, and intelligence.

I suggest that it is only through reason and revelation, as Heavenly Father intends, that we can know of Him and about Him. It all comes down to how diligently we seek after Him to experience Him.

As we begin our search, He gives us a little here and a little there, with things growing brighter and brighter. He gives us something and then waits on us to comprehend the revelation of additional truth to see what we will do with it. Then he gives us more. We begin to truly know Him, to see Him as a God of love, divinity, and glory, as revealed through modern revelation.

Chapter 8
Our Loving Father in Heaven

"The Christian does not think God will love us because we are good, but that God will make us good because He loves us."[79]

What is Heavenly Father's glory? What does it mean to be a son and daughter of the Man of Holiness? How deep and penetrating is God's love for me?

If I have learned anything in life, it is that you *never* give up on someone. The Savior in the Garden of Gethsemane descended below all things to comprehend all things so that He could perfectly relate to anyone in the direst situation, no matter how ugly, dark, or depressing. He did this so that He could heal and lift us to greater heights, which He will do one day for all of us. The Father and the Son, two perfect beings of love, never give up on anyone.

To illustrate my point, let me introduce Team Hoyt: Dick Hoyt and his son Rick.[80] This father-and-son team has competed together in more than 225 triathlons, 22 duathlons, 72 marathons, and many other long-distance races. Dick pulls his son in a boat as they swim, carries his son in a seat in the front of a bicycle, and pushes his son in a wheelchair as they run.

Rick Hoyt was born with his umbilical cord around his neck, blocking oxygen flow to his brain, resulting in cerebral palsy. Rick was born in 1962. At that time, people with special needs were institutionalized. The doctors told Rick's parents that their son would be a vegetable. But Rick's parents, Judy and Dick, noticed Rick's eyes following them around the room. This gave them hope.

Every week, Rick's parents took him to the Children's Hospital in Boston. One doctor there encouraged them to treat Rick like any other child. Judy spent hours each day teaching Rick the alphabet with sandpaper letters and posting signs on objects around the house. And Rick began to learn. At elven, Rick was given a computer to help him communicate. Over time, he graduated from Boston University and later worked in a computer lab developing communications systems for people with disabilities.

Team Hoyt began when Rick asked his father if they could run in a race together to benefit a lacrosse player at his school who had become paralyzed. Dick was not a runner. But they finished the five-mile race. Afterward, Rick said, "Dad, when I'm running, it feels like I'm not handicapped." Dick began running every day with a bag of cement in the wheelchair when Rick was at school or was studying and unable to train with him. As of April 2014, Team Hoyt had competed in 1,108 endurance events.

Much like Team Hoyt, Heavenly Father and the Savior carry us through our struggles in life. Though we can merit little on our own, They love us enough to carry us through anyway.

Modern Revelation—Our Greatest Source on Heavenly Father's Love

Though we have many evidences that God is real and exists as our Father in Heaven, modern-day revelation teaches us much more about Him. Through this revelation, we learn of His divine nature, expanding dominions, glory, power, and light of His intelligence—as the most supremely intelligent being. Abraham 3:19 reads, "I am the Lord thy God, I am more intelligent than they all."

The LDS conception of God is powerful. We learn from modern revelation that our Heavenly Father has within all the powers of life, intelligence, truth, and glory. They are part of His being, as well as a product of His mind. Heavenly Father is the supreme intelligence. He is the power by which all things were created in heaven or earth—a gift from Heavenly Father and made to come to pass through Christ. As Paul taught, "For by him were all things created, that are in heaven, and that are in earth, visible and invisible, whether they be thrones, or dominions, or principalities, or powers: all things were created by him, and for him: and he is before all things, and by him all things consist" (Colossians 1:16–17).

These are only a few of the traits and characteristics of our Heavenly Father. In the great plan of eternity, we are treading in His path. He holds all power, comprehends all things, and possesses a fulness of all light, truth, intelligence, and power that dwells eternally within Him. Joseph Smith said of Heavenly Father that he "sittest enthroned, with glory, honor, power, majesty, might, dominion, truth, justice, judgment, mercy, and an infinity of fulness, from everlasting to everlasting" (D&C 109:77).

In scripture, Heavenly Father is referred to by several titles that describe His greatness and glory. One of the most frequent titles is Man of Holiness. In the book of Moses, Enoch wrote, "Behold, I am God; Man of Holiness is my name; Man of Counsel is my name; and Endless and Eternal is my name, also" (Moses 7:35). Christ referred to Himself as the Son of the Man of Holiness as a statement of His divine relationship to Heavenly Father. Other name titles include God Almighty, Endless, and Alpha and Omega.

Christ in His mortal ministry, where He lived perfectly with the daily travails of life in our fallen world, directed His disciples to look even beyond Him in the perfection of His love and attributes. "Why callest thou me good?" the Savior stated. "None is good, save one, that is, God" (Luke 18:19).

A God of Love: To Be in His Presence

Jewish apocryphal sources tell of Adam and Eve's intense desire to return to the Garden of Eden and feel the radiance of love that emanates from Heavenly Father's presence. In *The Life of Adam of Eve*,[81] Adam was dying near the end of his life. Eve desired to return to the Garden of Eden and fetch the healing oil of the tree of life to administer to her lifelong companion. No longer innocent and living in a fallen world, Adam's and Eve's experiences in the Garden of Eden were sweet memories of walking with Heavenly Father in the coolness of paradise.

To put this into perspective, life in a terrestrial garden pales in comparison to our former celestial home, just as the brightness of the moon pales in comparison to the glorious radiance of the sun at noon. If Adam and Eve longed to be back in the paradisiacal Garden of Eden that was terrestrial in nature, just think of how we will long for our celestial home, bright and as beautiful as a flaming sun, when in the resurrection we remember life there.

Speaking of the aftermath of the First Vision theophany, Joseph Smith remarked to an acquaintance, "My soul was filled with love and for many days I could rejoice with great joy and the Lord was with me but I could find none that would believe the heavenly vision, nevertheless I pondered these things in my heart."[82]

Or on the road to Emmaus, two disciples walking along the dirt road with the Savior remarked after Christ revealed Himself to them, "Did not our heart burn within us" (Luke 24:32). They felt light and glory from the Savior, though it was confined within His newly resurrected physical tabernacle, who had just received the keys of the universe from Heavenly Father.

Though the scriptures speak profoundly of God's love, Heavenly Father has been classified as a god of wrath and vengeance, or as a distant or uncaring God. In his sermon "Sinners in the Hands of an Angry God," theologian Jonathan Edwards characterized Heavenly Father as, "The God that holds you over the pit of hell, much as one holds a spider or some loathsome insect over the fire, abhors you, and is dreadfully provoked. His wrath toward you burns like fire."[83] John Calvin wrote, "God preordained, for His own glory and the display of His attributes of mercy and justice, a part of the human race, without any merit of their own, to eternal salvation, and another part, in just punishment of their sin, to eternal damnation."[84] Saint Augustine created the paradox that God did not begin to love us until Christ died for us. But modern revelation reminds us, "Ye were also in the beginning with the Father" (D&C 93:23), and surely He loved us there because we are "[His] work and [His] glory" (Moses 1:39).

Heavenly Father is a God of love. "He that loveth not knoweth not God; for God is love," testified the Apostle John (1 John 4:8). He then said, "In this was manifested the love of God toward us, because that God sent his only begotten Son into the world, that we might live through him" (verse 9). King Benjamin talked of his personal knowledge of "the goodness of God, and His matchless power, and His wisdom, and His patience, and His long-suffering towards the children of men" (Mosiah 4:6). Or as Job mused, "What is man, that thou shouldest . . . set thine heart upon him?" (Job 7:17).

Yet with all our failings and imperfections, God loves us infinitely, unfailingly, and perfectly. What does that say about our worth? If Heavenly Father loves us, shouldn't we love ourselves and our developing divine natures?

The Joys of His Eternal Life

Because He loves us, Heavenly Father wants us to return to Him. He desires that we become like Him and enjoy eternal existence as He does. He provides a richly abundant eternal life, if that is our choice. Though we are passing through difficulties in this mortal experience—a mere moment in an eternity of time—Heavenly Father holds out eternal joy for us, with all it's life-giving and celestial powers, desiring that we reach up and grasp it.

On a grand scale, Heavenly Father reaches out to us through love and compassion. But that love is only discernible to us when we turn to Him and experience Him, not just assume He is there. Just as we do not like to see those we love suffer, Heavenly Father in His infinite love—who notices everything about us through the power of His Spirit, even the whereabouts of sparrows—is not free from our emotional pain.

Conclusion

For a time, I served as a volunteer teaching a fatherhood class to inmates in a local jail. The curriculum helped men learn new skills and motivate them to be good fathers upon their release. I learned something of Heavenly Father's deep and personal love for all of us one day teaching the class.

That day, there was a man in the class who I had become acquainted with. He was in his early thirties and was a negligent father to nine children from nine different women. He only had contact with a few of these children. At the start of the class, I remember looking at him and thinking how irresponsible it was of him to leave nine children without a father. This was his first incarceration and his sentence was for about one year. In my one-on-one interactions with him, I saw he was sincere about changing his life.

Near the end of my lesson, he caught my eye. I looked right at him, and then the Spirit told me inside, *Tell him how I love him.* It was one of those spiritual experiences when time seems to slow down. I asked, seeking clarification, *Not that You love him, but* how *You love him?* The answer back was, *Yes, tell him* how *I love him.*

This wonderful feeling of love enveloped me, and I knew it was Heavenly Father giving me a degree of the love that He wanted this man and the others in the class to feel. I was taken back momentarily. Then I said to the class that I needed to change direction for a bit. I looked back in this man's face for a few seconds, and then at everyone in the room. I said, "I want you to know that God loves you. I hope you know that. But let me tell you *how* God loves you." Words filled my mind about their potentials as sons of God and how the power of the Atonement is the only real force available to us to make lasting changes. Tears of joy filled my eyes and the eyes of all the men seated in blue jumpsuits. Even in a jail, Heavenly Father can find us and express His love.

Heavenly Father seems determined to demonstrate that when we make regrettable choices, we are not really choosing what the better angels of our natures want to choose. He wants us to come and try again. "His hand is stretched out still" (Isaiah 10:4).

Chapter 9
The Relatable God

"Beauty itself is but the sensible image of the infinite."[85]

Through life's experiences and trials, can I really relate to God? If He is my Father, how am I like Him? Did I know about life's trials before I came here?

A grandfather, a holy man, was caring for his grandson and sent him out to play with the other children. Shortly, the boy returned sobbing as if his heart would break. He explained, "I was playing hide-and-seek with my friends. I went and hid and waited, but no one came for me. They all ran away." The grandfather embraced him and said, "Now you know how God feels. He hides, and no one comes for Him."

A vital and distinguishing characteristic of LDS doctrine is that Heavenly Father is a glorified, holy, perfected, resurrected man with a corporeal body, and we, His children, are like Him.

Joseph Smith revealed that God is a distinct, tangible being with a body similar in form and stature to that of humans. We read in Doctrine and Covenants 130:22, "The Father has a body of flesh and bones as tangible as man's; the Son also." In Doctrine and Covenants 93:33, we are taught, "The elements are eternal, and spirit and element, inseparably connected, receive a fulness of joy." This beautiful insight that the Father has a light-filled, glorified body of flesh and bones makes Him relatable to us, for one day we will be resurrected and return to His presence.

God is a tender-hearted parent, who yearns for us like earthly fathers and mothers do. But much of the religious world has reasoned away this important fact that ties us to Him. We can relate to a Heavenly Father who is like us. Elder Richard J. Maynes taught, "Being offspring of a loving Heavenly Father is such a basic principle of the gospel of Jesus Christ that even our children proclaim its truth as they sing the Primary song 'I Am a Child of God.' "[86]

Elder Russell M. Nelson said, "God is the Father of our spirits. He has a glorified, perfected body of flesh and bone. We lived with Him in heaven before we were born. And when He created us physically, we were created in the image of God, each with a personal body."[87]

We are like Heavenly Father in that we possess a physical body that is formed in His likeness and image. He has infinitely more intelligence and experience as an organized being than we do, but nonetheless He is our Father, and we are created in His image. Joseph Smith revealed that "though God, like man, is a corporeal being, He is free from the corrupt elements that are associated with man's physical body, by which the latter is subject to the many weaknesses and deficiencies of mortal existence."[88]

As Greek philosophy infiltrated early Church teachings, it was reasoned that God could not have a body of flesh and bones as tangible as a human's body. The Greeks viewed matter, the elements of the earth, as inherently corrupt and anything but divine. Therefore, how could God have a material body, He being holy, righteous, and all-good?

Greeks mythology is a fascinating pantheon of gods and goddesses with passions and personalities similar to humans. These gods were benevolent, treacherous, dishonest, immoral, and so on. Some gods were powerful, such as Poseidon, the god of the sea and earthquakes; Zeus, the god of the sky and thunder; or Athena, the goddess of wisdom. But eventually, the Greeks began to believe in a supreme God, who they reasoned was all-powerful, and possessed all wisdom and perfections in their absolute forms.

The Greeks articulated that if this supreme being is perfect, and perfection (being the ultimate form of itself) does not change, then God does not change. Nor could this absolutely perfected God be influenced by humanlike emotions or feelings because that would require some degree of change. The god of the Greeks was above that. The supreme god of the Greek philosophers was unchangeable in his perfected attributes and unlike and unconcerned with flawed human beings.

Unfortunately, this view of God has persisted through the ages, being accepted by the early Christian church fathers in the third and fourth centuries and passed down from generation to generation to some of churches today. So in our day, we find people indifferent to religion or believing in an all-powerful God or essence who presides over the universe and is the perfect embodiment of the moral good but is distant and unreachable.

In the New Testament, Christ commented, "Have I been so long time with you, and yet hast thou not known me, Philip? He that hath seen me hath seen the Father" (John 14:9). In His mortal life, all that Christ did was to honor the Father and reveal His true nature. Was Christ influenced by humanlike emotions or feelings? Was He unconcerned with flawed human beings? Did He not heal people and lift up the downtrodden? Even in the Garden of Gethsemane and on the cross, Christ was teaching us about Heavenly Father's nature to love all of His children.

To be like the Father during His mortal ministry—to manifest the character and attributes of the Man of Holiness—Christ acquired much of the Father's divine nature and glory prior to His time in mortality, going from grace to grace (as revealed by modern revelation). The Apostle John commented, "And I, John, saw that he received not of the fulness at the first, but received grace for grace; and he received not of the fulness at first, but continued from grace to grace, until he received a fulness; and thus he was called the Son of God, because he received not of the fulness at the first" (D&C 93:12).

However, to live as a mortal, Jesus, the carpenter from Nazareth, suppressed His divine nature to experience all the woes of mortality and the contrasts of pain and pleasure, joy and sadness, and so on so He could fully relate to us as we experience this world through our fallen natures. Of course He related to us in Gethsemane, but even in His daily walk, Christ descended below His divine nature to know the heights and depths of all existence. In other words, Christ suffered all to better relate to us, leading Him to the ultimate relating experience to us in the Garden of Gethsemane and becoming even more like the Father.

Another devastating blow to the true concept of a loving, related Heavenly Father was the politically driven, philosophically conceived Nicene and other councils that redefined God's physical and spiritual nature. In 325 AD, Emperor Constantine and the learned philosophers and churchmen of that day produced the Nicene Creed, which, 125 years later, became the Athanasian Creed. The issue of debate was "trinity in unity." Are the members of the Godhead separate and distinct beings or are They all one being? The Creed reads, "We declare the Father, Son, and Holy Ghost to be abstract, absolute, transcendent, imminent, consubstantial, coeternal, and unknowable, without body, parts, or passions and dwelling outside space and time." These councils produced the inescapable contradiction that the three members of the Godhead are separate beings but also a single being, creating the "mystery of the trinity."[89]

This creed and its distortion of the true nature of Heavenly Father has been taught through the ages. Elder Jeffery R. Holland taught,

> With such a confusing definition of God being imposed upon the church, little wonder that a fourth-century monk cried out, "Woe is me! They have taken my God away from me, . . . and I know not whom to adore or to address." . . .
>
> How *are* we to trust, love, worship, to say nothing of strive to be like, One who is incomprehensible and unknowable? What of Jesus's prayer to His Father in Heaven that "this is life eternal, that they might *know thee* the only true God, and Jesus Christ, whom *thou* hast sent"? . . .
>
> These various evolutions and iterations of creeds—and others to come over the centuries—declared the Father, Son, and Holy Ghost to be abstract, absolute, transcendent, immanent, consubstantial, coeternal, and unknowable, without body, parts, or passions and dwelling outside space and time. In such creeds all three members are separate persons, but they are a single being, the oft-noted "mystery of the trinity." They are three distinct persons, yet not three Gods but one. All three persons are incomprehensible, yet it is one God who is incomprehensible.[90]

Is it any wonder that people today are generally confused about the true nature of Father in Heaven or believe Him to be distant and incomprehensible?

The truth of the matter is He is the God of love, like the father of the returning prodigal who sees his son returning home a great way off. When we come back into Father in Heaven's presence, when He sees us, He will have compassion and run to us, fall on our necks, and kiss us.

Chapter 10
The Glory of God

> "The heavens declare the glory of God; and the firmament sheweth his handywork" (Psalm 19:1).

What is glory? What is the Father's divine nature? Why am I commanded to bring light unto my soul?

In C. S. Lewis's fiction for children, he hides away many beautiful metaphors about light and God's glory for readers to find.

In *The Voyage of the Dawn Treader*, Lucy, Edmund, Eustace, King Caspian, and Reepicheep (a fearless mouse) travel onboard a ship through the easternmost sea toward the end of the world—the edge of Aslan's country. As they sail on, the seascape begins to change. The sun increases to an almost unbearable brightness, but the temperature does not increase. As they approach, the sun appears three times larger, and then five and six times bigger. Next, Reepicheep jumps into what he thinks will be seawater, and Lewis wrote,

> But when the dripping Mouse had reached the deck it turned out not to be at all interested in the Sea People.
>
> "Sweet!" he cheeped. "Sweet, sweet!"
>
> "What are you talking about?" asked Drinian crossly. "And you needn't shake yourself all over *me*, either."
>
> "I tell you the water's sweet," said the Mouse. "Sweet, fresh. It isn't salt." . . .

> "Perhaps your Majesty would like to taste it first," said Drinian to Caspian.
>
> The King took the bucket in both hands, raised it to his lips, sipped, then drank deeply and raised his head. His face was changed. Not only his eyes but everything about him seemed to be brighter.
>
> "Yes," he said, "it is sweet. That's real water, that. I'm not sure that it isn't going to kill me. But it is the death I would have chosen—if I'd known about it till now."
>
> "What do you mean?" asked Edmund.
>
> "It—it's like light more than anything else," said Caspian.[91]

After partaking of the delightfully sweet and fresh water (or "light," as Prince Caspian pointed out), it heightens and intensifies the travelers' bodily senses and perceptions. They are better able to look into the blinding light of the enlarging sun and see even more of the beautiful scenery. They are able to even look right into the center of the shining sun and move beyond their world and glimpse where Aslan and his Father reside.

As the children, the prince, and the mouse travel on, they notice the sea becoming more and more shallow, with beautiful white lilies floating on the surface and intoxicating scents wafting through the air. Because the water level dropped significantly, the travelers go on by rowboat, with Lucy trying to contemplate the type of place a being of greatness such as Aslan would live in with his Father.

Next, the travelers see a beach and blue wall of water in perpetual motion that reaches and blends into the blueness of the sky. As they approach, the beach transforms into a green field of grass, where they see an object of exquisite, blinding brightness.

C. S. Lewis borrowed the phrase *light from behind the sun* from a friend to describe Christ's light, power, and glory, which Christ received from the Father by going from grace to grace. Lewis quoted poet Charles Williams: "A light that shone from behind the sun; the sun / Was not so fierce as to pierce where that light could."[92] As an extension of this idea, we learn from modern revelation that "this is the light of Christ. As also he is in the sun, and the light of the sun, and the power thereof by which it was made" (D&C 88:7). And we learn further, "The glory of God is intelligence, or, in other words, light and truth" (D&C 93:36).

The Ultimate Self-Esteem Booster: "Behold, Thou Art My Son"

In the scriptures, we read of a man who killed another man to save a slave's life. The dead man was a taskmaster who was beating a Hebrew slave. The man who killed the taskmaster buried the lifeless man in the desert sand and, fearing for his life, fled across the scorching Sinai Peninsula to Midian.

How did Heavenly Father approach this man? Did He angrily condemn him or afflict him with a punishment? No, Heavenly Father led him to safety and refuge, and lovingly nurtured him, with a refiner's fire, into the great prophet Moses.

To prepare Moses to write Genesis, the Lord appeared to Moses and revealed Moses's true identity as a son of God. "And God spake unto Moses, saying: Behold, I am the Lord God Almighty, and Endless is my name; for I am without beginning of days or end of years . . . behold, thou art my son" (Moses 1:3–4).

This impressed Moses. Again and again in Moses's account, he remarked how Heavenly Father called him "my son." Commenting on lessons learned from this experience, Bishop Richard C. Edgley taught, "Moses knew who he was, he knew who Heavenly Father and Jesus Christ were, and he knew the source of his strength."[93]

In the Pearl of Great Price account, Moses was privileged to glimpse Heavenly Father's divine nature through Christ's appearance to him. Moses actually described being transfigured for his mortal body to withstand the intense power of Heavenly Father's glory. Influenced by the light, intelligence, and power of the Father's glory, Moses actually "beheld the world and the ends thereof, and all the children of men which are, and which were created; of the same he greatly marveled and wondered" (Moses 1:8).

Incidentally, Moses was overshadowed with merely a portion of Heavenly Father's glory. This portion permitted Moses to see everything on the earth in a single glance. We know that Moses did not behold all of the Father's glory: "Wherefore, no man can behold all my works, except he behold all my glory; and no man can behold all my glory, and afterwards remain in the flesh on the earth" (verse 5).

Just think of Heavenly Father's powers and abilities manifested through all of His glory, power, might, and majesty. Imagine the things that we will be able to experience and accomplish as celestial resurrected beings.

After the vision closed and Heavenly Father's glory left Moses, he fell lifeless to the ground. Moses remarked, "Now . . . I know that man is nothing" (verse 10), *nothing* meaning powerless. We are everything to our Heavenly Father. Moses was commenting that all creation and life-sustaining light and power come from Heavenly Father, and man comparatively can do nothing himself.

After being in the presence of God and having His glory withdrawn, Moses was left to himself. Enervated, Moses fell to the earth unconscious. Moses did not regain his natural strength for many hours. Coming to himself, he remarked, "Mine own eyes have beheld God . . . for I should have withered and died in his presence; but his glory was upon me; and I beheld his face, for I was transfigured before him" (verse 11).

In Moses's weakened conditioned (and never one to miss an opportunity to strike), Satan appeared on the scene. "Moses, son of man, worship me" (verse 12). Moses asked Satan, "Who art thou? For behold, I am a son of God, in the similitude of his Only Begotten; and where is thy glory, that I should worship thee?" (verse 13).

Once known as the "light bearer" and "son of the morning," Lucifer's glory has dimmed drastically compared to his previous station in premortality. However, now as the prince of darkness, his spiritual body still has elements of light and possesses the ability to appear as an angel. From the New Testament: "for Satan himself is transformed into an angel of light" (2 Corinthians 11:14). From the Book of Mormon: "who transformeth himself nigh unto an angel of light, and stirreth up the children of men unto . . . all manner of secret works of darkness" (2 Nephi 9:9).

Compared to the glory of Christ or the Father, Satan and his followers have virtually no light, which Moses quickly surmised in his weakened condition after basking in Heavenly Father's glory. Upon discerning the noticeable difference in light and glory, Moses does not let up on Satan and challenges him. "Blessed be the name of my God, for his Spirit hath not altogether withdrawn from me, or else where is thy glory, for it is darkness unto me? And I can judge between thee and

God; for God said unto me: Worship God, for him only shalt thou serve" (Moses 1:15). Moses's boldness increased: "Get thee hence, Satan; deceive me not" (verse 16).

Then Satan lashed out. "Cry[ing] with a loud voice, and ranted upon the earth, and commanded, saying: I am the Only Begotten, worship me"(verse 19). Naturally, Moses was frightened and he saw the bitterness of hell. Moses prayed and received strength. He commanded Satan to depart. "Depart from me, Satan, for this one God only will I worship, which is the God of glory. And now Satan began to tremble, and the earth shook; and Moses received strength, and called upon God, saying: In the name of the Only Begotten, depart hence, Satan. And it came to pass that Satan cried with a loud voice, with weeping, and wailing, and gnashing of teeth; and he departed hence, even from the presence of Moses, that he beheld him not" (verse 20–22).

I cannot state emphatically enough, as with Moses, that you and I are daughters and sons of a God of glory, light, truth, light, and eternal power. What does that say about you?

With Heavenly Father's light and glory surrounding and enveloping him—elevating Moses to a higher plain of understanding, intelligence, and emotion—Moses was shown all the inhabitants of the earth and he "discerned them by the Spirit of God" (verse 28). Enoch was also privileged to see the same in vision "And it came to pass that the Lord showed unto Enoch all the inhabitants of the earth" (Moses 7:21). In the Book of Mormon: "And when the Lord had said these words, he showed unto the brother of Jared all the inhabitants of the earth which had been, and also all that would be; and he withheld them not from his sight, even unto the ends of the earth" (Ether 3:25).

However, the most descriptive account of the glory of Heavenly Father in scripture is perhaps from the Prophet Joseph Smith: "I saw a pillar of light exactly over my head, above the brightness of the sun, which descended gradually until it fell upon me. . . . When the light rested upon me I saw two Personages, whose brightness and glory defy all description" (Joseph Smith—History 1:16–17).

From statements given by the Prophet Joseph Smith, Elder Orson Pratt published the following account of the first vision.

> And while thus pouring out his soul, anxiously desiring an answer from God, he at length, saw a very bright and glorious light in the heavens

> above; which, at first, seemed to be a considerable distance. He continued praying, while the light appeared to be gradually descending towards him; and as it drew nearer, it increased in brightness and magnitude, so that, by the time that it reached the tops of the trees, the whole wilderness, for some distance around was illuminated in a most glorious and brilliant manner. He expected to have seen the leaves and boughs of the trees consumed, as soon as the light came in contact with them; but perceiving that it did not produce that effect, he was encouraged with the hope of being able to endure its presence. It continued descending slowly, until it rested upon the earth, . . . and he was enveloped in the midst of it. When it first came upon him, it produced a peculiar sensation throughout his whole system and immediately, his mind was caught away, from the natural objects with which he was surrounded; and he was enwrapped in a heavenly vision, and saw two glorious personages, who exactly resembled each other in their features or likeness.[94]

Resurrected beings also have glory, though not the same glory as that of the Father and the Son, who possess perfected divine natures. Oliver Cowdery described the angel Moroni's appearance to Joseph:

> The first sight was as though the house was filled with consuming and unquenchable fire. This sudden appearance of a light so bright, as must naturally be expected, occasioned a shock or sensation, visible to the extremities of the body. It was, however, followed with a calmness and serenity of mind, and an overwhelming rapture of joy that surpassed understanding, and in a moment a personage stood before him.
>
> Notwithstanding the room was previously filled with light above the brightness of the sun, as I have before described, yet there seemed to be an additional glory surrounding or accompanying this personage, which shone with an increased degree of brilliancy, of which he was in the midst; and though his countenance was as lightning, yet it was of a pleasing, innocent and glorious appearance, so much so, that every fear was banished from the heart, and nothing but calmness pervaded the soul but one touch with the finger of his love, yes, one ray of glory from the upper world, or one word from the mouth of the Savior, from the bosom of eternity, strikes it all into insignificance, and blots it forever from the mind.[95]

The light emanating from Heavenly Father and the Savior is Their glory, intelligence, and power, also known as the Spirit of Truth. "The light and the Redeemer of the world; the Spirit of truth, who came into the world, because the world was made by him, and in him was the life of men and the light of men" (D&C 93:9). This light is a physical substance called intelligence and truth, "which truth shineth. This is the light of Christ" (D&C 88:7).

That is why we have been commanded to receive the light of truth: "And every man whose spirit receiveth not the light is under condemnation" (D&C 93:32). "And if your eye be single to my glory, your whole bodies shall be filled with light, and there shall be no darkness in you; and that body which is filled with light comprehendeth all things" (D&C 88:67).

How does light enter into us? How do we receive it? Elder Bruce R. McConkie stated, "Christ is the light; the gospel is the light; the plan of salvation is the light; 'that which is of God is light; and he that receiveth light, and continueth in God, receiveth more light; and that light groweth brighter and brighter until the perfect day.' As the light of the sun enters the body *through our natural eyes*, so the light of heaven—the light of the Spirit which illuminates our souls—enters through our spiritual eyes."[96] President Joseph F. Smith said,

> Men and women should become settled in the truth, and *founded in the knowledge of the gospel*, depending upon no person for borrowed or reflected light, but trusting only upon the Holy Spirit, who is ever the same, shining forever and testifying to the individual and the priesthood, who live in harmony with the laws of the gospel, of the glory and the will of the Father. They will then have light everlasting which cannot be obscured. By its shining in their lives, they shall cause others to glorify God; and by their well-doing put to silence the ignorance of foolish men, and show forth the praises of him who hath called them out of darkness into his marvelous light.[97]

We Are to Receive Light and Truth

The Spirit of Truth is where Heavenly Father's omniscience, omnipotence, and omnipresence flow. Through our time on this earth and the resurrection, we acquire light and truth so we will be worthy to dwell in Heavenly Father's presence of light and truth. As Isaiah said, "Who among us shall dwell with everlasting burnings? He that walketh righteously, and speaketh uprightly. . . . He shall dwell on high" (Isaiah 33:14–16).

The Prophet Joseph Smith taught, "God Almighty Himself dwells in eternal fire . . . for all corruption is devoured by the fire. 'Our God is a consuming fire.' When our flesh is quickened by the Spirit, there will be no blood in this tabernacle. . . . Some dwell in higher glory than others."[98]

The Prophet Joseph saw in vision the reality of these everlasting burnings: "The heavens were opened upon us, and I beheld the celestial kingdom of God, and the glory thereof. . . . I saw the transcendent beauty of the gate through which the heirs of that kingdom will enter, which was like unto circling flames of fire; also the blazing throne of God" (D&C 137:1–3).

The Apostle John in Doctrine and Covenants taught how we may gain the light and glory of our Father in Heaven, which He desires to share with us: "He that keepeth his commandments receiveth truth and light, until he is glorified in truth and knoweth all things" (D&C 93:28). Therefore, glory is constituted of truth and light. John later taught that the glory of God is intelligence: "The glory of God is intelligence, or, in other words, light and truth" (verse 36).

Heavenly Father and the Savior possess bodies of flesh and bone, as tangible as a person's body. They have, centered in Their physical beings, glory—or living spiritual power or intelligence, which is a physical substance of light and truth. This glory is what Moses, Enoch, the brother of Jared, Joseph Smith, and other prophets have witnessed, which Joseph described as "above the brightness of the sun" (Joseph Smith—History 1:16).

One has only to look at the beauty and grandeur of the creations of the universe to know the greatness and our Heavenly Father's awesome powers of intellect. "Behold, all these are kingdoms, and any man who hath seen any or the least of these hath seen God moving in his majesty and power" (D&C 88:47).

Emanating through the Immensity of Space

Another part of Heavenly Father's glory, the essence of His person, is His Holy Spirit. This intelligent power and light emanates through the immensity of space: "Which light proceedeth forth from the presence of God to fill the immensity of space—the light which is in all things, which giveth life to all things, which is the law by which all things are governed, even the power of God who sitteth upon his throne, who is in the bosom of eternity, who is in the midst of all things" (D&C 88:12–13).

Through the powers of His Spirit, the Father is connected to all things He has created Himself or through the Son—worlds without number. This constitutes his omnipresence. Imagine what it must be like to look down on your creations and, through the interconnectedness you possess with the universe, receive light and intelligences back into your presence, simultaneously communicating to you the condition of all creatures, great and small, knowing their cares and concerns.

As His children, Heavenly Father's glory and divine nature are part of us. "The day shall come when you shall comprehend even God, being quickened in him and by him. Then shall ye know that ye have seen me, that I am, and that I am the true light that is in you, and that you are in me; otherwise ye could not abound" (D&C 88:49–50).

Elder Charles W. Penrose told us how we, as the Father's children, can see His glory and divine nature as it quickens and dwells in all things.

> This spirit which pervades all things, which is the light and life of all things, by which our Heavenly Father operates, by which He is omnipotent, never had a beginning and never will have an end. It is the light of truth; it is the spirit of intelligence. . . . When we look up to the heavens and behold the starry worlds, which are kingdoms, we behold God moving in His Majesty and in His power. . . . If you see a living blade of grass you see a manifestation of that Spirit which is called God. If you see an animal of any kind on the face of the earth having life, there is a manifestation of that Spirit. If you see a man you behold its most perfect earthly manifestation. And if you see a glorified man, a man who has passed through the various grades of being, who has overcome all things, who has been raised from the dead, who has been quickened by this spirit in its fulness, there you see manifested, in its perfection, this eternal, beginningless, endless spirit of intelligence. Such a Being is our Father and our God, and we are following in His footsteps.[99]

Heavenly Father's omniscience also arises from His divine nature and glory. It is the powers and interconnectedness of His Holy Spirit that communicates knowledge of all things throughout the immensity of space to Him. Christ shares this ability with the Father. Christ, speaking of Himself, said, "Thus saith the Lord your God, even Jesus Christ, the Great I am, Alpha and Omega, the beginning and the end, the same which looked upon the wide expanse of eternity, and all the seraphic hosts of heaven, before the world was made; the same which knoweth all things, for all things are present before mine eyes" (D&C 38:1–2). At this moment in eternity, we cannot see God in His bodily form, but He can see us. "Wherefore, I can stretch forth mine hands and hold all the creations which I have made; and mine eye can pierce them also" (Moses 7:36).

Omniscience is an important attribute of our Father in Heaven, relative to our salvation. Joseph Smith commented, "Without the knowledge of all things God would not be able to save any portion of his creatures. For it is the knowledge which he has of all things from the beginning to the end that enables him to give that understanding to his creatures by which they are made partakers of eternal life. And if it were not for the idea existing in the minds of men that God has all knowledge, it would be impossible for them to exercise faith in him."[100]

Conclusion

Heavenly Father, the Man of Holiness, desires that we His children learn to live in a similar manner to His existence. He desires that we partake of His divine nature and bring light and glory into our spiritual organizations.

It is His work and glory to bring to pass the immortality and eternal life of His children and help us realize the joy of our redemption. Joy is the heavenly homecoming. We catch moments of happiness in this life. But only when we return to our heavenly home, after passing through the darkness of a telestial world, will we experience joy—the joy of becoming more like our Father in Heaven and Christ. We will know that Heavenly Father has always been there for us, lovingly encouraging us along the path of eternal progression.

Much of the religious world believes that God created us from nothing. If this were the case, and God being all-good, logically He would have created us perfected like He is. But even Heavenly Father could not create us perfect like Him. Instead, He instilled within us a spark of divinity and instructed us in light and glory in the premortal existence. Then He sent us to a fallen world to grow from opportunities to realize our divine potential.

And on our harrowing journey, it takes a God to respect our freedom in this world and withhold Himself from rushing in to prevent the consequences of that freedom in this vitally instructive period of our development. Yes, He created the earth, but He created an earth according to divine law, where people could exercise their freedom and progress through suffering to reach a higher state of perfection and happiness.

He loves and assists us throughout a premortality, mortality, and postmortality until all have fully had the opportunity to become more like Him and enjoy His creative, progressive eternal life.

Chapter 11
I Stand All Amazed at Christ

"Then knowledge through our Lord and Savior Jesus Christ is the grand key that unlocks the glories and mysteries of the kingdom of heaven."[101]

Who is the Savior? What does it mean, He went from grace to grace? How does the Son dwell in the Father? How did Christ become as the Father?

In my mind's eye, I like to try and visualize certain important and emotional scenes from the scriptures. Here's one such glimpse from my vantage point.

Yeshua walked slowly up into the hills, His back to the city. The night was heavy, the darkness palatable and ominous at the edges. As He passed through the Gate of the Essenes, He thought about how within the city walls they were plotting to kill Him. He knew it would be at the hands of the Roman soldiers at Golgotha, the place of the skull, by crucifixion.

From the stony hills, He stopped to look over His shoulder at the lights around the temple and down at the roofs of the houses where people slept, unaware of what He would do for them that night. The lights around the temple, illuminated by vats of olive oil on stilts and ignited with fire, made Him remember teaching there; the little children beaming with innocence and His sincere disciples and friends listening intently, which always gladdened His heart. He continued on the dirt path and glanced up the hill to Gethsemane in the distance.

Yeshua stopped again and looked over His shoulder at Jerusalem. A memory came to mind, of Him walking through the sheep market at the pool of Bethesda and asking the man, afflicted for thirty-eight years, to rise, and the tears and look of unfailing gratitude on the man's worn face. The memory still brought joy to Yeshua. To feel another wave of joy as He walked to Gethsemane, He thought of entering the city of Nain and the woman weeping there, her only son laid on a bier, being carried out for burial, as He commanded the young man to arise. He remembered the widowed mother's joy at the return of her son. Yeshua's eyes filled with tears. His mind moved forward in time. Next, He remembered the sadness and incredulity in Mary's face, noticing where the tears had rolled down her dust-covered cheeks and her words, "If thou hadst been here, my brother had not died."

The incline of the dusty paths through the hills up to Gethsemane continued to ascend. Looking across the hills, Yeshua remembered Nazareth as a boy, with the sloping green hills of the springs and the wildflowers blooming on the hillsides. The sweet memories of childhood. He thought of His mother, Mary, her sadness when Joseph died, and her telling Yeshua that she need His help now more than ever. He remembered how He felt more alone than ever with His stepfather gone.

Reaching the gate to the garden, Yeshua asked Peter, James, and John to wait for Him about a stone's cast. He knelt near a large stone buried in the earth. "Father," He prayed. "If thou be willing, remove this cup from me: nevertheless not my will, but thine be done"

An angel appeared from heaven, strengthening Him. In His consciousness, mortal time ceased. In vision, He could see the first earth He had created for the Father and then found Himself in a garden paradise. A lone man wandered into the scene of the vision. Yeshua beheld the man's face and instantly knew him intimately. The man's pains, sorrows, griefs, sicknesses, transgressions, self-doubts, disappointments, fears, loneliness, and sins left him and entered into Yeshua, and He felt them deeply, down inside His soul, suffering both physical and mental anguish. As He took upon Himself the whole of this man, tears of empathy streamed down His cheeks. Yeshua noticed He was sweating red. He shuddered under the weight of what was to come.

The Power of the Atonement: I Stand All Amazed

"I Stand All Amazed" gives us a sense of the awe and wonder the hymn's author and composer, Charles H. Gabriel (1856–1932), felt for the Atonement of Christ. (For the text, see *Hymns*, no. 193.)

When was the last time you were truly amazed by something? In the hymn, as Charles H. Gabriel contemplates Christ's Atonement, he moves to amazement at the gift of Christ to all mankind. Then Gabriel searches for understanding of the depths of the Christ's love. He becomes confused, bewildered. It's too much to comprehend. He moves from the cerebral contemplation of the mechanics of the Atonement to the emotional love of Christ, causing reverberations in his heart as he trembles to know that Christ was personally crucified, suffered, bled, and died for him. The power and awesomeness of the Atonement, and his dependency upon it, dawns on Gabriel in the full brightness of a morning sun and causes a physical reaction.

Christ desires to save you, love you, cleanse you, and heal you to make you happy. It is an overpowering desire in His nature. He has a desire to save you and call you His. This desire is more than we can comprehend. It is infinite. I invite you to move in His direction and start to feel His love. Let that work within you. As Elder David A. Bednar taught, "It is one thing to know that Jesus Christ came to earth to *die* for us—that is fundamental and foundational to the doctrine of Christ. But we also need to appreciate that the Lord desires, through His Atonement and by the power of the Holy Ghost, to *live* in us—not only to direct us but also to empower us."[102]

You have the power to reach out and emotionally affect Christ and add to His joy and happiness. Yes, you have that ability and relationship. When we show appreciation for the Savior in our thoughts, kind gestures to others, searches into the mysteries of godliness, service in His temple, and so on, this brings Him joy. If we choose not to accept and live the gospel, the Savior regrets that choice but loves us still.

"Jesus wept"

In my opinion, one of the most important scriptures is in the New Testament: "Jesus wept" (John 11:35). These two words give insight into the emotional dimensions of the Savior's personality as a being full of love. In the scriptures, He is moved to tears at the suffering and plight of others, an indicator of His empathy that would be perfected in its absolute fulness in Gethsemane.

Word had reached Christ that Lazarus was dead. Lazarus had been dead for four days. The New Testament reports that many Jews "came to Martha and Mary, to comfort them concerning their brother" (John 11:19). When Martha heard that Christ was coming, she went out of the small village to meet Him. Upon finding the Savior, in what must have been heartfelt pain and suffering at the passing of her beloved brother, she said, "Lord, if thou hadst been here, my brother had not died. But I know, that even now, whatsoever thou wilt ask of God, God will give it thee" (verses 21–22). Jesus replied, "Thy brother shall rise again" (verse 23), to which Martha said, "I know that he shall rise again in the resurrection at the last day" (verse 24).

Then Christ taught that He is "the resurrection, and the life: he that believeth in me, though he were dead, yet shall he live: And whosoever liveth and believeth in me shall never die" (verses 25–26). Then he asked Martha if she believes this. She replied, "Yea, Lord: I believe that thou art the Christ, the Son of God, which should come into the world" (verse 27).

Martha called for Mary secretly and told her, "The Master is come, and calleth for thee" (verse 28). Still on the outskirts of the village, Mary "arose quickly, and came unto him" (verse 29). The Jews who had come to comfort and were sitting in her house when Mary left followed after her. With these people in tow, they witnessed Mary as she "fell down at his feet, saying unto him, Lord, if thou hadst been here, my brother had not died" (verse 32).

The scriptures tenderly report, "When Jesus therefore saw her weeping, and the Jews also weeping which came with her, he groaned in the spirit, and was troubled, and said, Where have ye laid him? They said unto him, Lord, come and see" (verses 33–34). Then, "Jesus wept" (verse 35). The Jews, seeing this, said, "Behold how he loved him!" (verse 36).

To understand the poignancy of the situation, you need to have experienced the death of a loved one. Christ had experienced that at least once with the death of his stepfather, Joseph. I myself lost a daughter when she was seventeen, and I know that immediately following the death of a loved one that there is a range of deep, painful, and heartfelt emotion. Jesus could see His friends whom He loved suffering, and it moved Him to tears.

The Choice to Love

As mortals, we may choose to not love fully or not to love at all. Some do this because the potential of rejection and emotional pain is too great. What if we extend and express our love to someone and they rejected us or make fun of us? Sometimes we love conditionally, deciding to love someone only when they act in certain ways. When the other meets those conditions, extending part of themselves to us, we return the love. When those conditions are not met, we feel justified in not loving that person in return, thereby protecting ourselves in a cocoon of justification.

The Savior, however, takes on the possible and actual rejection for all of us. He loves us despite the fact that His love may not be returned. He loves us endlessly, even when we turn a cold shoulder to Him. "His hand is stretched out still" (Isaiah 9:21). And He has "graven thee upon the palms of my hands; thy walls are continually before me" (Isaiah 49:16).

Like the Savior, Heavenly Father knew from the beginning that some of His children would reject Him. But He loves us all anyway in the face of the rejection. When Lucifer and his followers were cast out of heaven, the heavenly hosts did not say good riddance; they wept.

Love is the defining characteristic of heaven. President J. Reuben Clark Jr., a former attorney general who was well acquainted with the laws of justice and mercy, expressed his belief "that our Heavenly Father wants to save every one of his children. I do not think he intends to shut any of us off because of some slight transgression, some slight failure to observe some rule or regulation. . . . I believe that in his justice and mercy, he will give us the maximum reward for our acts, give us all that he can give, and in the reverse, I believe that he will impose upon us the minimum penalty which it is possible for him to impose."[103]

Chapter 12
The Eternal Freedom We Gained in Gethsemane

"The cumulative weight of all mortal sins—past, present, and future—pressed upon that perfect, sinless, and sensitive Soul!"[104]

How is Christ the only source of real change? How does spiritual death cut me off from the powers of life? How does Christ open the way for me to acquire divine powers?

President Gordon B. Hinckley relayed the following modern-day parable that takes place in a one-room schoolhouse in the mountains of Virginia, where the boys were so rough no teacher had been able run the school.[105]

> One day an inexperienced young teacher applied. He was told that every teacher had received an awful beating, but the teacher accepted the risk. The first day of school the teacher asked the boys to establish their own rules and the penalty for breaking the rules. The class came up with 10 rules, which were written on the blackboard. Then the teacher asked, "What shall we do with one who breaks the rules?"
>
> "Beat him across the back ten times without his coat on," came the response.
>
> A day or so later, . . . the lunch of a big student, named Tom, was stolen. The thief was located—a little hungry fellow, about ten years old.
>
> As Little Jim came up to take his licking, he pleaded to keep his coat on. "Take your coat off," the teacher said. "You helped make the rules!"

> The boy took off the coat. He had no shirt and revealed a bony little crippled body. As the teacher hesitated with the rod, Big Tom jumped to his feet and volunteered to take the boy's licking.
>
> "Very well, there is a certain law that one can become a substitute for another. Are you all agreed?" the teacher asked.
>
> After five strokes across Tom's back, the rod broke. The class was sobbing. Little Jim had reached up and caught Tom with both arms around his neck.
>
> "Tom, I'm sorry that I stole your lunch, but I was awful hungry. Tom, I will love you till I die for taking my licking for me! Yes, I will love you forever!"

Spiritual Death—Losing Powers of Life

Sin captivates and binds the light and goodness within human souls. We become captive to it, "according to the captivity of the devil, and also according to the justice of God, upon all those who will work wickedness and abomination before him" (1 Nephi 14:4).

Sin binds us physically with addictions and habits, as well as mentally and emotionally. In this world, we all fall. We let go of our divine natures that we come here with—our powers of spiritual life—making us more susceptible to sin. In a vision, Enoch beheld "Satan; and he had a great chain in his hand, and it veiled the whole face of the earth with darkness; and he looked up and laughed, and his angels rejoiced" (Moses 7:26). In more subtle imagery, Nephi taught, "The devil . . . is the founder of . . . works of darkness; yea, and he leadeth them by the neck with a flaxen cord, until he bindeth them with his strong cords forever" (2 Nephi 26:22).

In Gethsemane, the Lord took upon Himself all your chains. This includes your sins, transgressions, ungodly desires, weaknesses—everything that binds and leads you captive to Satan. Then, under the tremendous weight of this captivity, He broke free from those chains, emerging from darkness into light. That means you can be made free through repentance. The Book of Mormon prophet Alma taught, "The Son of God suffereth according to the flesh that he might take upon him the sins of his people, that he might blot out their transgressions according to the power of his deliverance" (Alma 7:13).

The Savior not only took upon himself the fallen nature you inherited by being born into this world but also your spiritual inadequacies created from your sinful desires and choices. And we are also all free from physical death because the Savior's Atonement covers the transgression of Adam and Eve, which brought death into the world.

Suffering our spiritual deaths, His invitation to all is to come unto Him and take full advantage of the newness of life that only He offers. As Paul taught the Romans, "As Christ was raised up from the dead by the glory of the Father, even so we also should walk in newness of life" (Romans 6:4).

When we break ourselves against any of the commandments, we are violating divine law, and our spiritual bodies lose light and luster. As the Book of Mormon teaches, "Yea, he shall die as to things pertaining unto righteousness" (Alma 12:16). The prophet Jacob taught that "spiritual death is hell" (2 Nephi 9:12). In this process of taking our individual spiritual deaths upon Him, Christ "descended below all things, in that he comprehended all things, that he might be in all and through all things, the light of truth" (D&C 88:6). This not only qualified Him to empathize with us but also to develop a future fulness of light and truth in us.

The Garden of the Olive Press

The Garden of Gethsemane was aptly named. Gethsemane means "place of the olive press," which inspired English metaphysical poet and priest George Herbert to write, "Ev'n God himself being pressed for my sake."[106]

In Christ's day, people would place sheets under the olive trees and beat the trees to remove the olives. They would gather the fruit and place it in an olive crusher, a large wheel-shaped stone in a basin. Under the pressure of the stone, the skin and fleshy parts of the hard olives burst open. The crushed olives were then collected in mash sacks and taken to the olive press, which consisted of a heavy press beam and round pressing board. Large stones weighed down the beam and pressed the olive oil out of the mash sacks, where it would ooze into vats.

In Gethsemane, the metaphors of beating, crushing, and pressing the olives comes to life. Christ suffered alongside us, exactly as we suffer from our sins. He suffered the precise spiritual death we heap upon ourselves, sin by sin. Because of this, He is an active participant in our lives. The Savior does not merely give us good life advice, standing at a distance, uninvolved in the actual suffering. The Savior's Atonement is personal. Just think of the perfect empathy. As an infinite being, and having gone through the ordeal of Gethsemane for us, Christ knows us better than we know ourselves. Can you feel another person's emotional pains from sins, sufferings, and sicknesses? Not only can the Savior feel these things precisely as we feel them, He knows how to relieve our sinful burdens, healing us from within.

Elder Merrill J. Batemen wrote,

> Just as the lame man at the pool of Bethesda needed someone stronger than himself to be healed (see John 5:1–9), so we are dependent on the miracles of Christ's atonement if our souls are to be made whole from grief, sorrow, and sin. If grieving parents and loved ones have faith in the Savior and his plan, death's sting is softened as Jesus bears the believers' grief and comforts them through the Holy Spirit. Through Christ, broken hearts are mended and peace replaces anxiety and sorrow. . . . As Isaiah stated concerning the Savior, "Surely he hath borne our griefs, and carried our sorrows. . . . And with his stripes we are healed" (Isaiah 53:4–5).[107]

The Only Source of Real Change

The Atonement is about so much more than the forgiveness of sin. We beat ourselves up over our sinful natures. Even Nephi was guilty of this: "Nevertheless, notwithstanding the great goodness of the Lord, in showing me his great and marvelous works, my heart exclaimeth: O wretched man that I am! Yea, my heart sorroweth because of my flesh; my soul grieveth because of mine iniquities" (2 Nephi 4:17).

The Atonement will never be fully understood by us mortals. Its full effects are beyond mortal comprehension. Yet we should do everything in our power to understand the powers and effects of the Atonement as we "search deeper and deeper into the mysteries of godliness."[108]

Two theories on the Atonement offer insight. The moral influence theory states that through contemplating Christ's suffering for us, our hearts turn naturally to Him and we are filled with divine love and power that transforms us into new creatures in Christ. The ransom theory depicts God as being offended at our sins and demanding retribution or satisfaction. Yet we mortals are required to forgive one another without requiring retribution or satisfaction. So why wouldn't God, especially if we have turned our hearts to Him? The ransom theory seems to put justice and mercy above God.

Whatever theory is most correct, the real purpose of the Atonement is lasting change that, through Christ, restores and enhances our light-filled divine natures. All human will combined is but a drop of perspiration compared to the beautiful, surging, blue ocean of the Atonement.

Like stars falling from orbit, we lose our luster in this fallen world. It comes with the telestial territory in this mortal sphere of existence. The fall we all take by coming to this benighted world will be for our benefit through the Savior's Atonement and grace, and it will ignite more and more light in us until the perfect day.

The life-giving powers of the Atonement restore luster that we brought with us to this life and prepare us to receive more light in the next life. In regards to this truth, Robert L. Millet, emeritus dean of religious education at Brigham Young University, wrote,

> One who chooses Christ chooses to be changed. . . . The Atonement is the means whereby our hearts might be cleansed and our souls transformed and prepared to dwell with Christ and our Eternal Father. . . . The Atonement does more than fix the mistakes. It does more than balance the scales. It even does more than forgive our sins. It rehabilitates, regenerates, renews, and transforms human nature. Christ makes us better, worlds better, than we would have been had there been no Fall.[109]

On the same theme, Elder Tad R. Callister remarked, "The Atonement was designed to do more than restore us to the starting line—more than just wipe the slate clean. [Its] crowning purpose [is] to endow us with power so that we might overcome each of our weaknesses and acquire the divine traits that would make us like God."[110]

The Atonement Is Personal—It's about You!

The prophet Isaiah declared, "When thou shalt make his soul an offering for sin, he shall see his seed" (Isaiah 53:10). In a similar vein, the prophet Abinadi also prophesied, "When his soul has been made an offering for sin he shall see his seed" (Mosiah 15:10).

Who is the Savior's seed? And when will He see His seed?

His seed is us, followers of Christ who are doing our best to add light to our divine natures and become His sons and daughters.

When did He see us, His seed?

He beheld us when His soul was made as an offering for sin. That occurred in two places, the Garden of Gethsemane and on the cross. In the Garden of Gethsemane, He saw us as He took up Him our sinful natures to give us the hope of restoring and adding to our divine natures. And He saw us when He was on the cross. Elder Merrill J. Batemen said, "In the garden and on the cross, Jesus saw each of us and not only bore our sins, but also experienced our deepest feelings so that he would know how to comfort and strengthen us."[111]

In part, Christ earned His empathy for mortals through day-to-day living in His mortal ministry. But in the garden, He reached the pinnacle of relatedness to us, acquiring complete and perfect empathy. His Atonement for you is all about you! You cannot say to Him, "You don't understand. You don't know how I feel. You don't know how much this hurts."

Spiritual death is a form of spiritual alienation of the divine relationship that we can have with Father in Heaven. But it is more than a geographic banishment from God's presence. Just as the physical body weakens with disease, we are weakened spiritually as we embrace each new sin. Perhaps we lose our capacity or will to absorb light and truth. As with physical death, there must be some power to reverse the decaying process, heal our spiritual wounds, and strengthen our spiritual fiber. The Atonement is that reversing power.

Conclusion: An Infinite and Eternal Sacrifice

Christ was not like you and me in mortality. Christ was not only sinless but also had acquired a fulness of the Father's divine nature, consisting of Heavenly Father's intelligence, light, truth, and power (in addition to a host of other divine attributes). The Savior received additional endowments through His physical conception as the Only Begotten Son, which includes more of the Father's divine nature. By virtue of possessing these infinite and eternal qualities merited and inherited from the Father, Christ had the ability to make an infinite and eternal sacrifice for us by sacrificing these attributes.

By His consent, the Savior's divine power and attributes were withdrawn from Him in Gethsemane and may have been withheld from Him until He allowed Himself to die on the cross. According to President Brigham Young, "At the very moment, at the hour when the crisis came for Him to offer up His life, the Father withdrew Himself, withdrew His Spirit, and cast a vail over [Jesus]. That is what made Him sweat blood. If He had had the power of God upon Him, He would not have sweat blood; but all was withdrawn from Him, and a veil was cast over Him, and He then plead with the Father not to forsake Him."[112]

Without His divine attributes and power to protect Him, the sins, transgressions, pains, suffering, sorrowing, and so on of worlds without number were heaped upon His sinless soul. The totality of spiritual death and darkness wracked His soul mercilessly, tormenting Him and causing unfathomable emotional and physical pain in body and spirit. In this state, He descended below all things, retaining the awful experience in memory that He might succor us in our direst needs.

And then the ordeal was over. Christ emerged from the Atonement triumphant with healing in His wings. Because of Him, the effects of sin and error can be reversed and erased for all eternity so that we might live forever, infinitely and eternally, and acquire divine Christlike powers for ourselves.

Chapter 13
Titles for the Savior

"If Christ Jesus dwells in a man as his friend and noble leader, that man can endure all things, for Christ helps and strengthens us and never abandons us. He is a true friend."[113]

Who is Christ? Based on His many titles, what is His role in my life and the universe? Can I truly be like Him?

Jayne B. Malan, in her talk "Summer of the Lambs," reported that as a young girl she would spend summers on her family's ranch in Wyoming. One summer at the age of twelve, she and her brother Clay were given a heavy responsibility. A violent storm had killed many of her father's sheep, leaving 350 lambs without mothers.[114]

Sister Malan said, "To feed one or two baby animals is one thing, but to feed 350 is something else! It was hard. There was plenty of grass, but the lambs couldn't eat the grass. They didn't have teeth. They needed milk."

Jayne and her brother made V-shaped feeding troughs out of boards. Then they made a thin mash of milk and grain. "I rounded up the lambs, herded them to the troughs, and said, 'Eat!' Well, they just stood there looking at me. Although they were hungry and there was food in front of them, they still wouldn't eat."

Soon the lambs began starving to death. "The only way we could be sure they were being fed was to pick them up in our arms, two at a time, and feed them like babies. And then there were the coyotes. At night the coyotes would sit up on the hill, and they'd howl. The next morning we would see the results of their night's work, and we would have two or three more lambs to bury."

Jayne and her brother had to dispose of the dead lambs. She said of this, "I got used to that . . . until I named one of the lambs. It was an awkward little thing with a black spot on its nose. It was always under my feet, and it knew my voice. I loved my lamb. It was one I held in my arms and fed with a bottle like a baby. One morning my lamb didn't come when I called. I found it later that day under the willows by the creek. It was dead. With tears streaming down my face, I picked up my lamb and went to find my father. Looking up at him, I said, 'Dad, isn't there someone who can help us feed our lambs?'

Wisely, her father responded, "Once a long, long time ago, someone else said almost those same words. He said, 'Feed my lambs. . . . Feed my sheep. . . . Feed my sheep.' "

The Savior is the one who can save us all! As the scriptures teach, "Mine Only Begotten Son, who is full of grace and truth, which is Jesus Christ, the only name which shall be given under heaven, whereby salvation shall come unto the children of men" (Moses 6:52).

Titles for the Savior

Jesus Christ is known by many titles, including Savior, Redeemer, Jehovah, The Great I Am, Advocate, and Mediator of the New Covenant. Elder Lawrence E. Corbridge taught, "Jesus Christ is the Way. He is Light and Life, Bread and Water, the Beginning and the End, the Resurrection and the Life, the Savior of the world, the Truth, and the Way. There is only one way to happiness and fulfillment. He is the Way. Every other way, any other way, whatever other way, is foolishness."[115]

This is powerfully taught in the Doctrine and Covenants: "he who came unto his own was not comprehended. The light shineth in darkness, and the darkness comprehendeth it not; nevertheless, the day shall come when you shall comprehend even God, being quickened in him and by him. Then shall ye know that ye have seen me, that I am, and that I am the true light that is in you, and that you are in me; otherwise ye could not abound" (D&C 88:48–50).

Christ's Relationship to the Father: From Grace to Grace

Christ is everything He is because of the Father. The glory and power of the Father dwell in Christ, and it is through Christ that people receive the powers of life and light as benevolent gifts from the Father. All things relating to life and eternal progress for us—past, present, and future—come from Christ, as dictated by the Father. This is why He said, "Why callest thou me good? none is good, save one, that is, God" (Luke 18:19).

The Apostle John testified, "I, John, saw that he received not of the fulness [of the Father's glory] at the first, but received grace for grace; and he received not of the fulness at first, but continued from grace to grace, until he received a fulness" (D&C 93:12–13).

To receive of the Father's fulness is to receive endowments of His glory, light, intelligence, and power. The Savior received these spiritual endowments as He gave grace for grace in service to us in premortality. As a mark of His character, the Savior covenanted with the Father to consecrate the glory, light, intelligence, and power received and develop it in us, Father in Heaven's other children. Through the vast ages of premortality, Christ continued from grace to grace, giving of Himself in service to us through creating worlds and leading the work of salvation and exaltation. As He did this, He acquired more and more of the Father's glory.

His culminating act of grace to receive the complete fulness was to work out the Atonement for all of His creations upon which Heavenly Father's children dwell and give His life to usher in resurrection upon all these worlds. Then the Father gave the Savior a fulness of the attributes and powers of eternal life—all the Father possessed.

In Palestine, Christ said, "Be ye therefore perfect, even as your Father which is in heaven is perfect" (Matthew 5:48), with no mention of Himself. However, to the Nephites after His Resurrection, He could now point to Himself with the Father as a perfect and holy being we should model ourselves after: "I would that ye should be perfect even as I, or your Father who is in heaven is perfect" (3 Nephi 12:48).

Of the resurrected Christ, the Prophet Joseph Smith wrote that He possesses "the same mind, the same wisdom, glory, power, and fulness—filling all in all,"[116] as the Father. "Filling all in all" refers to how Christ, through His divine nature is in all things, "comprehendeth all things, and all things are before him, and all things are round about him; and he is above all things, and in all things, and is through all things, and is round about all things; and all things are by him, and of him, even God, forever and ever" (D&C 88:41).

Perfectly United: The Indwelling Relationship

The Apostle John explained how Christ received a fulness of the Father's divine nature, which created an indwelling relationship: "And the glory of the Father was with him, for he [the Father] dwelt in him" (D&C 93:17). Christ said to the Nephites, "I am in the Father, and the Father in me; and in me hath the Father glorified his name" (3 Nephi 9:15).

The *Lectures on Faith* teach how the Father's glory is centered in Christ: "The Father and the Son possessing the same mind, the same wisdom, glory, power and fulness—filling all in all, the Son being filled with the fulness of the mind, glory, and power; or, in other words, the Spirit, glory, and power of the Father, possessing all knowledge and glory, and the same kingdom, sitting at the right hand of power, in the express image and likeness of the Father—a Mediator for man—being filled with the fulness of the mind of the Father; or, in other words, the Spirit of the Father."[117]

The Savior taught the prophet Ether, "Behold, I am he who was prepared from the foundation of the world to redeem my people. Behold, I am Jesus Christ. I am the Father and the Son. In me shall all mankind have life, and that eternally, even they who shall believe on my name; and they shall become my sons and my daughters" (Ether 3:14).

Abinadi explained, "I would that ye should understand that God himself shall come down among the children of men, and shall redeem his people. And because he dwelleth in flesh he shall be called the Son of God, and having subjected the flesh to the will of the Father, being the Father and the Son—the Father, because he was conceived by the power of God; and the Son, because of the flesh; thus becoming the Father and Son—and they are one God, yea, the very Eternal Father of heaven and of earth" (Mosiah 15:1–4).

The Spirit of Truth emanates from the presence of God. Besides being part of the divine nature of the Father, the Spirit of Truth is also centered in Christ. Through the eons of time in premortality, the Spirit of Truth was developed in Christ until he received a fulness grace for grace. Through the Spirit of Truth, Christ shares the Father's thoughts, glory, and power as if the intelligence of the Father is in the body or personage of the Son. The Father, in His glory, possesses an interconnected relationship with all His creations.

In the scriptures, we learn that truth is a substance. It is light and glory and intelligence. This glorified substance, the Spirit of Truth, emanates from God as a glorified being to fill the immensity of space. This same Spirit of Truth is instilled in the Savior. He possesses the mind, glory, and power of the Father. This is what gives the Son all power in heaven and on earth. Additionally, as two glorified beings, They are perfectly unified and united as one, each possessing the same divine mind as the other.

In premortality, speaking of Christ's knowledge of the future that He acquired as He came to possess the Spirit of Truth in its fulness, the Prophet Joseph Smith said,

> The great Jehovah contemplated the whole of the events connected with the earth, pertaining to the plan of salvation, before it rolled into existence, or ever "the morning stars sang together" for joy [Job 38:7]; the past, the present, and the future were and are, with Him, one eternal "now;" He knew of the fall of Adam, the iniquities of the antediluvians, of the depth of iniquity that would be connected with the human family, their weakness and strength, their power and glory, apostasies, their crimes, their righteousness and iniquity; He comprehended the fall of man, and his redemption; He knew the plan of salvation and pointed it out; he was acquainted with the situation of all nations and with their destiny; He ordered all things according to the counsel of His own will; He knows the situation of both the living and the dead, and has made ample provision for their redemption, according to their several circumstances, and the laws of the kingdom of God, whether in this world, or in the world to come.[118]

Referring to how the Father and Son possess the same mind, President Brigham Young explained that while Christ was on earth, He talked with His Father and "dwelt in his bosom, and knew all about heaven, about making the earth, about the transgression of man, and what would redeem the people, and that he was the character who was to redeem the sons of earth, and the earth itself from all sin that had come upon it."[119]

Speaking on the unified relationship of the Father and the Son, the Prophet Joseph Smith asked, "Why was he [Christ] perfect? Because he was the Son of God, and had the fulness of the Spirit, and greater power than any man."[120]

The Light of Christ

The Light of Christ is derived from the Father's glory, light, intelligence, and power. As these spiritual substances dwell in Him, they are the source of the Light of Christ. Through the Father's divine nature, Jesus Christ is the Light and the Life of the World. "He that ascended up on high, as also he descended below all things, in that he comprehended all things, that he might be in all and through all things, the light of truth; which truth shineth. This is the light of Christ" (D&C 88:6).

The scriptures teach that the Light of Christ is "the light which is in all things, which giveth life to all things, which is the law by which all things are governed, even the power of God who sitteth upon his throne, who is in the bosom of eternity, who is in the midst of all things" (D&C 88:13).

Speaking of Christ, Doctrine and Covenants 88:7–12 revealed,

> As also he is in the sun, and the light of the sun, and the power thereof by which it was made. As also he is in the moon, and is the light of the moon, and the power thereof by which it was made; as also the light of the stars, and the power thereof by which they were made; and the earth also, and the power thereof, even the earth upon which you stand. And the light which shineth, which giveth you light, is through him who enlighteneth your eyes, which is the same light that quickeneth your understandings; which light proceedeth forth from the presence of God to fill the immensity of space.

In other words, the Light of Christ is the glory of God. It is the Holy Spirit that reaches out through all of Christ's creations. It is how Christ and the Father observe and control Their creations and sustain life and bless you and me.

Christ as the Only Begotten

Through Christ's conception as the Only Begotten of the Father, He received additional abilities and physical characteristics of the Father, the Man of Holiness. This is in addition to the indwelling relationship of how the Father's glory, light, intelligence, and powers were developed in Christ to where He came to possess them in their fulness.

In becoming the Only Begotten, Christ received a body of flesh to enable Him to become like the Father and perform the Atonement for all His creations. As the Only Begotten of the Father, He received in His mortal body the physical characteristics of perfection from the Father. From His mortal mother, He received mortal attributes so that He could experience the temptations and challenges of mortal life.

His conception was not like ours. He was conceived as the literal son of God with special powers to enable Him while in the flesh to manifest the Father to us and demonstrate the Father's perfections, love, and goodness through the indwelling relationship of Their glory. As the Only Begotten, Christ could truly call Himself the Son of the Most High God. Additionally, when Christ performed miracles or taught the people it was as if both the Father and the Son jointly performed the miracle or spoke forth the truth. This gives perspective to why "at the ninth hour Jesus cried with a loud voice, saying, Eloi, Eloi, lama sabachthani? which is, being interpreted, My God, my God, why hast thou forsaken me?" (Mark 15:27) when the Father's presence departed from Christ while He was on the cross—a necessary step in the final act of Atonement.

Church members sometimes teach that Christ was a dual being, part God and part fallen mortal. The prophet Abinidi taught, "God himself should come down among the children of men, and take upon him the form of man, and go forth in mighty power upon the face of the earth" (Mark 13:34).

Christ was a God during His mortal ministry. However, to experience mortality as we experience it, Christ suppressed His divine nature as a God. This allowed Him to experience the effects of the Fall we experience, such as pain, hunger, loneliness, temptation, sorrow, and ultimately death. As Alma taught, "And he will take upon him death, that he may loose the bands of death which bind his people; and he will take upon him their infirmities, that his bowels may be filled with mercy, according to the flesh, that he may know according to the flesh how to succor his people according to their infirmities" (Alma 7:12).

Conclusion: Acquiring the Divine Nature through Christ

Through the Atonement, men and women who have come unto Christ are given spiritual powers in mortality to benefit from Christ's indwelling relationship with the Father and His being the Only Begotten of the Father. This life is not only about being forgiven of sins we commit. We may receive of Christ's life-giving light to transform our fallen natures. "Therefore if any man be in Christ, he is a new creature: old things are passed away; behold, all things are become new" (2 Corinthians 5:17). The Savior promised, "But unto him that keepeth my commandments I will give the mysteries of my kingdom, and the same shall be in him a well of living water, springing up unto everlasting life" (D&C 63:23).

In other words, Christ is able, with our participation, to return us to a heightened spiritual state beyond our current fallen natures. Through the act of a God taking our fallen natures upon Himself, He helps us rise to higher levels of joy and righteousness as His spirit light, truth, and intelligence enters into us. The ultimate divine aid comes with help to keep highest commandment of all: "be perfect even as I, or your Father who is in heaven is perfect" (3 Nephi 12:48).

Often this commandment seems unattainable for us who are beset with so many failings and proclivities to sin. But we misread this commandment, thinking that the burden of perfection is on our shoulders. The message of the scripture is that there is an abundance of spiritual powers availed to us. We can only be made perfect through the Light and regenerating powers of Christ as we strive to do our best to live His gospel. We need the supernatural powers of heaven. We must rely on Christ as the Light and Life of the World as we did in premortality as we also progressed from grace to grace in our own way. Just as Christ received an eternal fulness from the Father by going from grace to grace, we too can go from grace to grace in this life and receive a fulness from our Father in Heaven.

President Brigham Young said,

> This life is worth as much to us as any life in the eternities of the Gods. . . . We are urged by the Spirit to refrain from articles which tend to death, to preserve this life, which is the most precious life given to mortal beings preparatory to an immortal life. It is our business to prepare to live here to do good. Instead of crying to the people prepare to die, our cry is prepare to live forevermore. These mortal houses will drop off sometime, and when they are cleansed and purified, sanctified and glorified, we shall inherit them again forever and ever. Let all the Saints pursue a course to live.[121]

It is Heavenly Father's object and design for His children to receive light and truth. There is so much inside us waiting to be discovered and pulled out in this mortal trial and experience. Through the Father and Son, we are truly remarkable beings.

Chapter 14
Christ's Blessings and Their Infinite Implications, Part 1

"Every good gift and every perfect gift is from above, and cometh down from the Father of lights, with whom is no variableness, neither shadow of turning" (James 1:17).

What does Christ's Atonement make possible for me? How does Christ redeem me and set me free from spiritual death? How does Christ make eternal life possible for me?

A parable from C. S. Lewis:

> Imagine yourself as a living house. God comes in to rebuild that house. At first, perhaps, you can understand what He is doing. He is getting the drains right and stopping the leaks in the roof and so on; you knew that those jobs needed doing and so you are not surprised. But presently He starts knocking the house about in a way that hurts abominably and does not seem to make any sense. What on earth is He up to? The explanation is that He is building quite a different house from the one you thought of—throwing out a new wing here, putting on an extra floor there, running up towers, making courtyards. You thought you were being made into a decent little cottage: but He is building a palace. He intends to come and live in it Himself.[122]

This chapter and the following two chapters list the many blessings and gifts available to us through the Atonement. Let's start with the Savior's overwhelming desire to bless us.

An Overwhelming Desire to Bless You

As the Prophet Alma taught, "And now, I ask, what great blessings has he bestowed upon us? Can ye tell?" (Alma 26:2).

The Lord wants to bless us in so many ways, all stemming from His desire to renovate us into magnificent palaces for the Spirit, light, glory, life, and truth of the Godhead to more abundantly reside.

During one period of Book of Mormon history, "so many [were] the blessings which were poured out upon the people, that even the high priests and the teachers were themselves astonished beyond measure" (Helaman 3:25). Blessings also extend from us to our posterity. "And, inasmuch as they are faithful, I will multiply blessings upon them and their seed after them, even a multiplicity of blessings" (D&C 104:33).

President James E. Faust taught of gospel blessings,

> Even though, as a man or a woman, we are born, live a brief moment, and then die, through the Atonement of Jesus Christ we will all live after death. Through the divinity which is within us as a gift of the great Creator, we can come to complete fruition as heirs of God with eternal powers, dominions, and progression without end. Paul said this gift is a free gift. Through the Mediation and Atonement we will be resurrected ourselves without going through any part of the atoning agony that the Son of God went through.[123]

Besides helping us to overcome the effects of spiritual death and setting our feet firmly on the clearly marked path to eternal exaltation, the Savior makes possible other blessings that impacted us before, during, and after this life.

Perfect Empathy so He Can Perfectly Relate to Us

Christ gives us the gift of perfect empathy. He not only suffered for our sins but also experienced our griefs and sorrows, so He perfectly empathizes with and relate to us. As Isaiah taught, "Surely he hath borne our griefs, and carried our sorrows: yet we did esteem him stricken, smitten of God, and afflicted. But he was wounded for our transgressions, he was bruised for our iniquities . . . and with his stripes we are healed" (Isaiah 53:4–5).

One title for Christ is Son of Man. This title is used eighty times in the Gospels alone when the Savior speaks of Himself. He is one of us, yet He was godlike in His mortality. He is representative of the ideal man, perfectly obedient to the Father at the head of the entire human family.

An angel asked Nephi, "Knowest thou the condescension of God?" He answered that he did not know the meaning of all things. To wit the angel replied, "Behold, the virgin whom thou seest is the mother of the Son of God, after the manner of the flesh" (1 Nephi 11:16, 18).

Christ condescended to this telestial state to experience mortality as we experience it to possess a perfect empathy and tread where we tread in this fallen world of contrasts, including light and darkness, pleasure and pain, and so on. He grew tired, became hungry, experienced loneliness and heartbreak, became sick, had headaches, tripped, and dealt with small-minded and offensive people.

He descended from His divine throne so that His "bowels [were] filled with mercy, according to the flesh, that he may know according to the flesh how to succor his people according to their infirmities" (Alma 7:12). He left a realm of celestial light for a dark and benighted world. Talk about contrasts. Yet He gladly did it. Was His entry into our world more difficult for Him because of how holy and good He was upon entering this fallen world?

Christ's empathy infinitely ranges from the beaming innocence of a child with Down syndrome—whose only desire is to love like Christ loves us—to the ostensibly bottomless chasm of darkness and despair bludgeoned into the lives of millions by a Hitler, a Stalin, or a Pol Pot.

Provides Purpose and Meaning to Mortal Life

At times, there is drudgery in this fallen world, where we live with the spiritual, physical, emotional and psychological effects of the Fall. When we come unto Christ, He heals us of these afflictions. Beyond that, He provides meaning and purpose to our struggles, with a promise of eternal life.

Just think of all a person learns and experiences in mortality, all a person sees and feels and comprehends, from infancy through death. This is all because of Christ!

From the moment we emerge as newborn babes and strain at the strange bright light of this world, we begin a journey of experiences. We feel emotions of love and fear, exhilaration and disappointment, joy and sadness, anger and serenity, and a host of other feelings. We come to know the thrill of Christmas mornings when young, the incomparable feeling of being in love for the first time, and the elation of accomplishing something great.

When you are first cradled in your mother's arms, you feel love and warmth, and then as you grow under the care of this beautiful other being with soft eyes and hair (almost goddess-like to us), she makes all things right, and you feel safe when the outside world frightens you. But then that outside world is full of adventure when you step into the buzzing green world of insects and birds within the safe enclosures of your backyard in springtime. Then as you get older and some independence, you are shipped off to school, where you begin to learn more of the world, form friendships, and live in a world of reality and play.

But then you grow and those childhood dreams and occupations no longer interest you. Your body changes and you enter a confusing world, stuck halfway between adulthood and childhood, and you experience new desire for independence and love, start to form a better sense of who you are, and push back against your parents and their rules and what they expect of you. In this new stage of life, you experience the power of love and attraction as you fall in and out of love and taste the desire for someone who is beautiful to you and makes you feel good about yourself—pulling you even further away from your parents and family. Then you make a commitment to that other person who makes life wonderful and grand—you get married and bring children into the world whom you love. Life becomes harder than it has ever been before, caring for little ones, and you learn to really love your spouse with a deepening love built on sacrifice for one another and your children. And then the years roll on, and you grow old together and experience even more of the world. But then one of you dies, and you feel the ache of loneliness from the absence of the person you spent almost every day with almost all of your life, giving and sacrificing together.

This is made possible because of the plan of salvation and the creation of the earth as a place of testing and probation, where we create our own libraries of experiences. In this life, we gain experiences through exercise of agency, which involves sins and transgression. Christ atones for the sins and overcomes these consequences, upon condition of repentance, and we are left with the experiences, truly knowing good from evil.

Eve proclaimed, "Were it not for our transgression we never should have had seed, and never should have known good and evil, and the joy of our redemption, and the eternal life which God giveth unto all the obedient" (Moses 5:11).

Power to Lift Us to Lift Themselves

The powers of the Atonement also include lifting us to loftier heights, to motivate us to change, even if we exercise only a particle of faith. Like a gravitational force present everywhere in the universe, the Atonement is reaching out to your best self, hoping, longing, and waiting for you to open your heart. As Nephi taught, "He doeth not anything save it be for the benefit of the world . . . even that he layeth down his own life that he may draw all men unto him" (2 Nephi 26:24). President Charles Penrose made the point that "if we really do believe in God and in Jesus Christ . . . the desire will enter our hearts to turn away from sin."[124]

The nature of the Atonement, when we reflect on it, moves us to sympathy, thus generating a mighty change of heart that brings us to higher ground spiritually, intellectually, and even physically with the refining and renovating powers of the Holy Ghost.

The Atonement paid for our sins, transgressions, mistakes, misdeeds, trespasses, offenses, infractions, and more—committed consciously or unconsciously—if we accept Christ's gift, come unto Him, and repent of our sins.

Without this gift, mankind would be in a never-ending downward spiral. Christ pays our debt to justice so we can stand on new ground and move forward in positive directions.

The Savior asked, "What manner of men [and women] ought ye *to be*? Verily I say unto you, even as *I am*" (3 Nephi 27:27; emphasis added). How is that even possible? Even Nephi, the man who beheld glorious visions and became a prophet, struggled. "O wretched man that I am! Yea, my heart sorroweth because of my flesh; my soul grieveth because of mine iniquities" (2 Nephi 4:17). Yet knowing Abraham was mortal, the Lord appeared to him and said, "I am the Almighty God; walk before me, and be thou perfect" (Genesis 17:1).

The Lord appeared to Abraham and made great promises to him, such as that his posterity would be as numberless of the stars of the heaven—an allusion to light-filled celestial bodies.

But before these promises would be fulfilled, Abraham was commanded to be perfect before the Lord. The Lord desires to confer the same blessings of Abraham upon us. Therefore, we must come unto Christ for our blessings.

But are we left alone to try our best to be obedient and earn these blessing all by our weak, mortal, fallen selves? Would the Lord give Abraham (and you and me) a command that is not possible to achieve? Would He not provide the means for accomplishing what He desires: for us to come unto Him and return to His celestial presence?

We are not left alone in mortality. Just as with Abraham, we are given an endowment of the Holy Spirit. President Lorenzo Snow taught, "Through that Gospel he [Abraham] could obtain that divine aid which would enable him to understand the things of God, and without it no man could arrive at a state of perfection before the Lord. So in reference to the Latter-day Saints, they could not possibly come up to such a moral and spiritual standard except through supernatural aid and assistance."[125]

As we come unto Him, the Lord provides the supernatural means to help us overcome ourselves and the world.

But how does Christ reach us to give us the supernatural means, or spiritual gifts, that lead us to exaltation with Him? The answer is in the cross.

Was it necessary that Christ's mortal life end on the cross? Did He need to be lifted up and die that way: nailed to wooden crossbeams, hanging there to die, nearly naked in humiliation? After completing the Atonement, could He have lived out the remainder of His days and die of natural causes? Setting aside the necessity of the Resurrection, why did Christ allow Himself to be lifted up for the world to see?

As a resurrected being, Christ said to the Nephites, "My Father sent me that I might be lifted up upon the cross . . . that I might draw all men unto me, that as I have been lifted up by men even so should men be lifted up by the Father, to stand before me, to be judged of their works, whether they be good or whether they be evil" (3 Nephi 27:14).

The imagery of dying on the cross is powerful. Once we understand how He, who was without sin or fault, was condemned to die so horrifically, the unfairness evokes our heartfelt sympathy. Religious people all the world over are deeply affected by the suffering of Christ.

He could have called down angels, yet He chose to submit and suffer unimaginable pain. Why? To reach us.

From the cross, Christ seems to be saying, "I am your fellow sufferer. I choose to suffer for you out of love. I am vulnerable also to the suffering brought on by your choices and the realities of this universe we inhabit that we are progressing through together, to become more like our Father in Heaven."

As gravity pulled His body down on the cross, the pain from the spikes in His wrists, hands, and ankles must have been excruciating. If He relaxed His legs, the weight of the Savior's body would pull down on His wrists, pressing the bones on the spikes. If the pain on the wrist bones become too much, Christ would have had to shift His weight up, tearing through the tissues of His feet and scraping His already lacerated back along the rough wood of the cross. The bleeding from open wounds would have caused dehydration and intense thirst.

Eventually, crucifixion causes the lungs to fill with fluid, compressing the heart to the point that it can beat no as longer or it bursts—a broken heart.

But His heart gladdened. A vision opened to Him. From the cross, he saw us, His family. As stated earlier, the vision Christ had on the cross was of all those who would become His sons and daughters through His great redemptive act. The prophet Isaiah declared that "when thou shalt make his soul an offering for sin, he shall see his seed" Isaiah 53:10). Abinadi prophesied, "When his soul has been made an offering for sin he shall see his seed" (Mosiah 15:10).

On a wall in the small hut where civil rights leader Gandhi lived hung a print of Christ with the inscription, "He is our peace." Christ, in the act of crucifixion, was wearing a loincloth, the same kind worn by millions of poor men oppressed in Indian villages. The similarity in dress between Christ and these men whom Gandhi was suffering for touched him. The first time Ghandi saw a life-size crucifix was in the Vatican in 1931. Of the experience, he said, "I saw there, many nations, like individuals, could only be made through the agony of the cross and no other way. Joy comes not by the infliction of pain on others, but the pain voluntarily borne by oneself."[126]

Imprisoned in Yervada jail, Gandhi was asked, "Isn't your fasting a species of coercion?" "Yes," he said, "the same kind of coercion which Jesus exercised upon you from the cross."[127]

At another time, Gandhi said, "What should a nonviolent person do when he finds his friends, relations, or countrymen refuse to give up an immoral way of life, and all arguments prove futile to evoke any response? . . . The first step is gentle and affectionate persuasion. When it fails to produce any salutary effect, voluntarily he invites suffering in his own body to open the eyes of the person who is determined to see no light."[128]

But because of the Savior, we don't need to go on a hunger strike or hang on a cross to reach those around us who are hurting themselves with poor choices. We have the example of the Master to follow. We can live Christlike lives. We can do all in our power to serve and sacrifice for those we love, as He has done. Service and sacrifice entail suffering, maybe in small degrees, but they require us to give something of ourselves.

On an infinitely smaller scale, a friend named Brett Folkman taught me about willingly suffering with others. Brett had entered the MTC on his way to South Africa. An elder in his district doubted whether he had a testimony of the Church and if he could serve a mission. Most of us would tell the struggling elder to pray and fast and God would give him an answer, and then go on our merry way, thinking about ourselves. Brett, however, said he wanted to pray and fast with him. In effect, Brett was saying, "Let us both humble ourselves before the Lord. I want to hunger and thirst after righteousness on your behalf." The elder received his answer and served a faithful mission. I often wonder, had Brett not suffered beside his fellow missionary, if the elder would have had the same experience.

The Savior has paid the price to the utmost farthing for you, opening up the way for you to have a better, more fulfilling life of real joy and insights into the divine within you. His invitation is for all to come unto Him. If you labor and are heavy laden, He gives you rest. Learn of Him, and you shall find rest. He encourages you to take His yoke upon you by going out and doing His works of service and compassion, and it will feel light.

Chapter 15
Christ's Blessings and Their Infinite Implications, Part 2

"If a son shall ask bread of any of you that is a father,
will he give him a stone? or if he ask a fish, will he
for a fish give him a serpent?" (Luke 11:11).

How is Christ the way? How does He sustain life as well as succor me day to day? How does Christ set all things right?

In the anonymous story *The Joy of Giving*, a woman who was traveling alone in the mountains found a precious stone in a stream. The next day, she met another traveler who was hungry, and the woman opened her bag to share her food. The hungry traveler saw the precious stone and asked the woman to give it to him. She did without hesitation. The traveler then left, rejoicing in his great fortune. He could see the stone was worth enough to give him security for a lifetime. But a few days later, he came back to return the stone to the woman. "I've been thinking," he said. "I know how valuable the stone is, but I give it back in the hope that you can give me something even more precious. Give me what you have within you that enabled you to give me the stone." The woman smiled and said, "The joy of giving."

Christ is the ultimate giver. We can develop within ourselves by coming unto Christ with those same desires to bless and give to others, as we are commanded to be like Him.

In the simple, metaphorical language of the New Testament, Jesus Christ described Himself as, to name a few, the Way, the Light and Life of the World, the Bread and Water, the Beginning and the End, the Resurrection and the Life, the Savior, and the Truth. However, undergirding these simple teachings are deep and far-reaching principles of eternal life available to all who love and follow the Savior.

He Created and Sustains Our Lives and All Life

Christ is the Creator. If there had been no Creation, there would be no mortal probation, and none of us would be progressing toward immortality and eternal life as promised in the scriptures. The beauty of the earth—the harmonized ecosystems, the seas teaming with life—would not exist. The scriptures teach that Christ, under Heavenly Father, is the master of these laws and forces of creation. "And I, God, said: Let the waters bring forth abundantly the moving creature that hath life, and fowl which may fly above the earth in the open firmament of heaven" (Moses 2:20).

If Christ did create these things, He clearly is master of the elements, down to their DNA structures. As the Master, all of creation obeys His voice. Because of Christ, this earth, from the directional forces of the smallest particle of DNA to the movements of stars and planets, all work in harmony and sustain life for us. Christ doesn't just understand the laws of creations; He makes them operational through the power and light of His divine nature. "As also he is in the sun, and the light of the sun, and the power thereof by which it was made. . . . And the earth also, and the power thereof, even the earth upon which you stand. . . . The light which is in all things, which giveth life to all things, which is the law by which all things are governed" (D&C 88:7, 10, 13).

Blessings of Succor

Another blessing of the Atonement is receiving of the Savior's succoring powers of healing and to feel his calming influence. Isaiah testified that Christ is "a strength to the needy in his distress, a refuge from the storm, a shadow from the heat" (Isaiah 25:4). For those who sorrow, Isaiah declared the Savior will "comfort all that mourn" (Isaiah 61:2), "wipe away tears from off all faces" (Isaiah 25:8), and "revive the spirit of the humble" (Isaiah 57:15).

When we surrender our wills to Christ, His Spirit heals us and rejuvenates hopelessness into hopefulness. Then His transformation of us takes place.

Alma the Younger was in need of renovating in his youth. By his own choices, he had become a miserable shack, darkened by denying the light for so long and even working to block the light so others could not receive it with his taunts and prideful jeers. After an angel awakened him to a sense of his awful guilt, Alma felt the full onslaught of self-torment that came with the realization of who he had become. "I was thus racked with torment, while I was harrowed up by the memory of my many sins" (Alma 36:17). A harrow is a type of rake with wooden spikes used to scrape and break through hardened soil. Alma said further of his experience,

> I remembered also to have heard my father prophesy unto the people concerning the coming of one Jesus Christ, a Son of God, to atone for the sins of the world. Now, as my mind caught hold upon this thought, I cried within my heart: O Jesus, thou Son of God, have mercy on me, who am in the gall of bitterness, and am encircled about by the everlasting chains of death. And now, behold, when I thought this, I could remember my pains no more; yea, I was harrowed up by the memory of my sins no more. And oh, what joy, and what marvelous light I did behold; yea, my soul was filled with joy as exceeding as was my pain!" (Alma 36:17–20)

But then, oh how did the Lord succor and nurture Alma.

He Sets All Things Right

A little girl—a beautiful, innocent ray of sunshine and goodness—could wander out into the street and a car could tragically strike and kill her. Through the Atonement, all the good, lovely, tender things that little girl would have created with her life will be made up to parents, siblings, and everyone close to her. The Prophet Joseph Smith taught that through the Atonement, the loss and promise of that life will be restored in the Lord's due time in an eternal way. He said, "All your losses will be made up to you in the resurrection, provided you continue faithful. By the vision of the Almighty I have seen it."[129] But how?

The light of the restored gospel says a mother and father, through temple sealing, will have their children with them for eternity, not just for a brief mortal span of a few decades. In this life, only by coming unto Christ can our grief find purpose and meaning. I know from experience, in quiet, personal moments, the inconsolable, crushing, suffocating grief that comes after losing a child. But with that grief, a soul-stretching experience comes.

Through Christ, the powers of Atonement open up more compassion and nobleness of soul, which bring peace in this life and a deep longing to be with that child eternally. You anxiously anticipate reuniting with that child. You feel his or her presence thinly through a veil of light, where that child can see through to you. You know somehow that your child is being cared for lovingly, perfectly, as he or she awaits you.

The gaping hole left open in our souls upon the departing of loved ones can be filled with the love of Christ if we allow the healing to flow inside us. After the initial shock of our loved ones being gone from this mortal sphere, slowly (based upon or readiness) the healing can flow.

As previously mentioned, the Prophet Joseph Smith taught, "All your losses will be made up to you in the resurrection, provided you continue faithful. By the vision of the Almighty I have seen it." Could Joseph have learned this from the vision recorded in Section 137 of the Doctrine and Covenants? "The heavens were opened upon us, and I beheld the celestial kingdom of God. . . . I saw . . . my brother Alvin, that has long since slept; and marveled how it was that he had obtained an inheritance in that kingdom" (D&C 137:1, 2, 5–6).

Alvin died at age twenty-five in 1823 from mercury poisoning, contracted from the medicine calomel given to him to help to cure a case of severe abdominal pain. Joseph was seventeen years old when Alvin died, and he adored his older brother. Joseph wrote, "I remember well the pangs of sorrow that swelled my youthful bosom and almost burst my tender heart when he died."[130] Joseph's mother recorded, "We all wept our irretrievable loss."[131]

Yes, through Christ we may have hope in this life that "all our losses will be made up to [us]" in the resurrection, with added blessings of increased powers of empathy and an enlarged capacity to feel joy from the light we bring into our lives. Additionally, besides in death, the Savior's Atonement sets other things right, even on a day-to-day level. The Savior's victory over death and sin compensates not only for our failings but also for our mistakes committed by errors in judgment and human inadequacies.

Conclusion: Eternal Families

An miraculous thing happened when Christ allowed Himself to die on the cross. The veil of the temple at Jerusalem was rent, symbolically suggesting that for all who follow Him that He will lead them through the veil of this world into celestial spheres, where God resides in a world of eternal splendor.

Through His temple ordinances, we are endowed to become eternal family units—the "nucleus of heaven,"[132] to borrow a phrase from the Prophet Joseph Smith—and given the power of eternal lives.

Only through Christ and His mastery over all things are eternal families sealed and bound together through righteousness for time and all eternity. Think of the joy of eternal life when you and your spouse have overcome the frailties and smallness of soul inherent in this mortal world and, through Christ, have become more like Him: full of grace, truth, beauty, and light. I cannot say it as well as the Lord has in D&C 132:19:

> And again, verily I say unto you, if a man marry a wife by my word, which is my law, and by the new and everlasting covenant. . . . Ye shall come forth in the first resurrection; and if it be after the first resurrection, in the next resurrection; and shall inherit thrones, kingdoms, principalities, and powers, dominions, all heights and depths . . . and they shall pass by the angels, and the gods, which are set there, to their exaltation and glory in all things, . . . which glory shall be a fulness and a continuation of the seeds forever and ever.

Chapter 16
Christ's Blessings and Their Infinite Implications, Part 3

"Even by the God of thy father, who shall help thee; and by the Almighty, who shall bless thee with blessings of heaven above, blessings of the deep that lieth under, blessings of the breasts, and of the womb" (Genesis 49:25).

How is Christ the only name under heaven that can save me? How can Christ overcome death and the effects of sin? What did Christ redeem me to become?

Elder Hugh B. Brown once told a story entitled "the Painter and the Child."[133]

> Centuries ago a great artist was engaged to paint a mural for the cathedral in a Sicilian town. The subject was the life of Christ. For many years the artist labored diligently, and finally the painting was finished except for the two most important figures: the Christ Child and Judas Iscariot. He searched far and wide for suitable models.
>
> One day while walking in the city he came upon some children playing in the street. Among them was a 12-year-old boy whose face stirred the painter's heart. The artist took the child home with him, and day after day the boy sat patiently until the face of the Christ Child was finished. But the painter still had found no model for the portrait of Judas.

The story of the unfinished masterpiece spread afar, and many men, fancying themselves of wicked countenance, offered to pose for Judas. But in vain the old painter looked for Judas, as he envisioned him—a man warped by life, enfeebled by surrender to greed and lust.

Then one afternoon as he sat in a tavern, a gaunt and tattered figure staggered across the threshold. "Wine, wine," he begged. The startled painter looked into a face that seemed to bear the marks of every sin of mankind. Greatly excited, the old painter said, "Come with me, and I will give you wine."

For many days the painter worked feverishly to complete his masterpiece. As the work went on, a change came over the model. A strange tension replaced the stuporous languor, and his bloodshot eyes were fixed with horror on the painted likeness of himself.

One day, perceiving his subject's agitation, the painter paused in his work. "My son," he said, "what troubles you so?"

The man buried his face in his hands, sobbing. After a long moment he lifted pleading eyes to the old painter's face. "Do you not then remember me? Years ago I was your model for the Christ Child."

He Restores Us to Innocence and Exalts Us to Higher Heights

The restored truths of the gospel are so profound and deep, beyond day-to-day living, on both religious and philosophical levels. It is no wonder that most people live with the generalities—though at times great insights burst through.

Perhaps because we can't see Him, we keep Christ at the periphery of our lives, when in actuality He is the source of the power, light, and knowledge of the solutions to our mortal cares. We sense the gospel depth on a subconscious level as it is woven into the fabric of reality, but the cares and distractions of the world (though trials are a necessary part of our development here in mortality) blur our focus on the profound specifics of our mortal experience and all that Christ makes possible for us.

I am not saying that only the relatively few souls who have a true knowledge of the Atonement understand all things or have a monopoly on meaning. Again, those people who wittingly or unwittingly live lives founded on Christ's principles of truth will find the most meaning, because He is the center of all things. "He comprehendeth all things, and all things are before him, and all things are round about him; and he is above all things, and in all things, and is through all things, and is round about all things; and all things are by him, and of him, even God, forever and ever" (D&C 88:41).

The principles and truths presented in this chapter demonstrate that Christ is more than a great teacher, like Buddha or Confucius. Did such great teachers of moral principles claim to be divine and the Son of God, promising rest, resurrection, and healing to all mankind through the Atonement? Christ cannot be reduced to a masterful teacher of the golden rule.

Christ is the Creator, the Light and Life of the World. He is the One upon whom our mortal and eternal happiness is dependent. Christ will save and redeem all men, women, and children, except the sons of perdition who have put themselves beyond His reach. Some Christian religions teach of an afterlife, but not many give details. They promise better lives in the world to come, often with only a mention of Christ, but not the understanding that the restored gospel of Jesus Christ can provide.

Christ is the only name given under heaven whereby mankind may be saved (see Acts 4:12). Once people begin to grasp their complete dependence on Christ, they can have an experience similar to the Book of Mormon people at the temple where Christ appeared, as recorded in 3 Nephi:

> And it came to pass that when Jesus had spoken these words the whole multitude fell to the earth; for they remembered that it had been prophesied among them that Christ should show himself unto them after his ascension into heaven. And it came to pass that the Lord spake unto them saying: Arise and come forth unto me, that ye may thrust your hands into my side, and also that ye may feel the prints of the nails in my hands and in my feet, that ye may know that I am the God of Israel, and the God of the whole earth, and have been slain for the sins of the world. (3 Nephi 11:12–14)

Then something interesting happened as these people, one by one, came forth and touched the sacred emblems of the Savior's body:

> And it came to pass that the multitude went forth, and thrust their hands into his side, and did feel the prints of the nails in his hands and in his feet; and this they did do, going forth one by one until they had all gone forth, and did see with their eyes and did feel with their hands, and did know of a surety and did bear record, that it was he, of whom it was written by the prophets, that should come. And when they had all gone forth and had witnessed for themselves, they did cry out with one accord, saying: Hosanna! Blessed be the name of the Most High God! And they did fall down at the feet of Jesus, and did worship him. (3 Nephi 11:15–17)

Hosanna is translated as "save us now." These people went from mental awareness that Jesus Christ is the Son of God to a testimony borne of the Spirit that He is the true Life and Light of the World. We can also know these things and touch the emblems every Sunday as we partake of the sacrament, putting the emblems inside our bodies, which one day He will resurrect that we will come up to the standard of our own perfections.

Overcomes Lucifer the Destroyer: The Resurrection and the Life

The prophet Jacob taught that if there we no Atonement, all men would be subject to "that awful monster the devil, and death, and hell, and that lake of fire and brimstone, which is endless torment" (2 Nephi 9:19). In other words, without the Atonement, we could not be forgiven for sins, healed emotionally or spiritually, or be resurrected and return to the presence of Heavenly Father. There would be no eternal life, exaltation, or families.

Jacob also taught, "Our spirits [would] become subject to . . . the devil, to rise no more. And our spirits [would] become like unto him, and we [would] become devils, angels to a devil, to be shut out from the presence of our God, . . . to remain with the father of lies, in misery" (2 Nephi 9:8–9).

Therefore, due to the demands of justice, we could not return to the Father's presence to partake of the degree of glory merited us through the gifts of grace extended by the divine Atonement. In other words, we would be prevented from returning to the Father's presence, "for all have sinned, and come short of the glory of God" (Romans 3:23).

However, through the Atonement, it is possible for men and women to be become clean and temporarily "quickened" so as to be able to withstand God's glory-filled presence. Joseph Smith taught that God "dwells in eternal fire; flesh and blood cannot go there, for all corruption is devoured by the fire."[134] Moses concurred from his real experiences with Christ representing the Father as he said, "God is a consuming fire" (Deuteronomy 4:24).

Regarding our mortal bodies, the prophet Jacob taught, "This flesh must have laid down to rot and to crumble to its mother earth" (2 Nephi 9:7). Paul, in writing to the Hebrews, said, "Him that had the power of death, that is, the devil" (Hebrews 2:14). It is not wonder that Satan is referred to as the destroyer.

But the power of resurrection has and will reverse the destructive forces of chaos and death as mortal flesh breaks down to return to its native element through entropy. "For as death hath passed upon all men, to fulfil the merciful plan of the great Creator, there must needs be a power of resurrection, and the resurrection must needs come unto man by reason of the fall; and the fall came by reason of transgression; and because man became fallen they were cut off from the presence of the Lord" (2 Nephi 9:6).

The sting of death is inescapable in this world, bringing with it heartache and soul-searching. American philosopher Ralph Waldo Emerson married Ellen Louisa Tucker in 1830 when she was eighteen. Already sick with tuberculosis, Ellen died at twenty on February 8, 1831. Her last words were, "I have not forgot the peace and joy."[135]

Emerson was devastated at the passing of his young wife, walking from Boston to her grave in Roxbury every day. In a journal entry more than one year after Ellen's passing, he recorded, "I visited Ellen's tomb and opened the coffin."[136] Contemporaries in Emerson's day had similarly opened their loved one's coffins, witnessing for themselves the seemingly permanent and inescapable nature of death. Yet the hope of resurrection is even greater that the sorrowful sting of death.

Ezekiel reported what he saw in vision:

> Then he said unto me, Son of man, these bones are the whole house of Israel: behold, they say, Our bones are dried, and our hope is lost: we are cut off for our parts. Therefore prophesy and say unto them, Thus

> saith the Lord God; behold, O my people, I will open your graves, and cause you to come up out of your graves, and bring you into the land of Israel. And ye shall know that I am the Lord, when I have opened your graves, O my people, and brought you up out of your graves, and shall put my spirit in you, and ye shall live, and I shall place you in your own land: then shall ye know that I the Lord have spoken it, and performed it, saith the Lord. (Ezekiel 37:11–14)

Christ is the Resurrection and the Life. Paul instructed Timothy, He "hath abolished death, and hath brought life and immortality to light through the gospel" (2 Timothy 1:10). Without Christ (as Jacob taught), "This flesh must have laid down to rot and to crumble to its mother earth, to rise no more" (2 Nephi 9:7). If Satan had not been defeated, there would be no resurrection, no breaking of the bands of death, and no coming forth from the grave. But because of the Atonement of Christ, all men will be raised from corruption to incorruption, from mortality to immortality, thereafter to live everlastingly in a resurrected state.

In other words, Christ reverses eternally the second law of thermodynamics and stops the decay interactions of chemical compounds that reduce protons into lighter particles. Christ's Atonement somehow changes our bodies to a state that is free from the entropic process. Contrasting a terrestial state with a celestial state—an immortal and terrestrial body, like Adam's in the Garden—it is exempt from decay and is not subject to disease, sickness, or pain. But a celestial (meaning resurrected and exalted) body has powers in direct opposition to entropy. As stated in Doctrine and Covenants 132, a celestial resurrected body has the powers of life, godhood, and creation, to name just a few.

In all grades of resurrection, from the telestial to the celestial, the countenance of a person will reflect the inner spiritual light that he or she collected to his or her soul.

> And the spirit and the body are the soul of man. And the resurrection from the dead is the redemption of the soul. And the redemption of the soul is through him that quickeneth all things. . . . And they who are not sanctified through the law which I have given unto you, even the law of Christ, must inherit another kingdom, even that of a terrestrial kingdom, or that of a telestial kingdom. For he who is not able to abide

> the law of a celestial kingdom cannot abide a celestial glory. And he who cannot abide the law of a terrestrial kingdom cannot abide a terrestrial glory. And he who cannot abide the law of a telestial kingdom cannot abide a telestial glory. (D&C 88:15–17, 21–24)

He Meets the Demands of Justice and Makes Repentance Possible

I had a teaching moment in the temple recently. I was performing baptisms for the dead with the youth from my ward. My eyesight was brought into sharp focus on the grip of hands on wrists of the person performing the baptism and the person receiving the ordinance.

My mind caught hold of how naturally the thumbs of both participants cover the center of each other's wrists. It is as if Christ, who is symbolically performing the ordinance, is saying to us, "By your willingness to be baptized and reach out and touch the token of the nail mark in my wrist, which is symbolic of my Atonement for the children of men, I promise to cover over—or protect you from—suffering for your sins because I make it possible for you to repent."

"For behold, I, God, have suffered these things for all, that they might not suffer if they would repent; but if they would not repent they must suffer even as I" (D&C 19:16–17). As Elder Neal A. Maxwell taught, "We will end up either choosing Christ's manner of living or His manner of suffering."[137]

The person receiving the ordinance of baptism also has his or her thumb over the Savior's wrist, in effect saying, "I will live my life in a way that I do not bring anymore pain or sorrow on to You, Lord, and do all I can to repent of my sins and transgressions through Your redeeming powers and grace, each week renewing this covenant."

Spiritual death is a form of spiritual alienation of the divine relationship that we can have with our Father in Heaven and the Savior. But it is more than a geographic banishment from God's presence. Just as the physical body weakens with disease, we are also weakened spiritually when we choose to sin. We lose our capacity or will to absorb light and truth. As with physical death, there needs to be some power to reverse the decaying process, to heal our spiritual wounds and strengthen our spiritual fiber. The Atonement is that reversing power.

Conclusion: Power to Gain Eternal Life

Because of the Lord Jesus Christ, we have power to gain eternal life, meaning living in the presence of our God. Just think of it! To live the glory-filled, endlessly joyful, creative, and masterful life of Father in Heaven, moving through the eternities with those we love in a state of perfection.

Doctrine and Covenants 76 is the blueprint for gaining eternal life for those people who have become sons and daughters of God, through the Atonement and by acquiring the attributes of Christ: "They are they who received the testimony of Jesus . . . and were baptized. . . . That by keeping the commandments they might be washed and cleansed from all their sins, and receive the Holy Spirit . . . who overcome by faith, and are sealed by the Holy Spirit of promise" (D&C 76:51–53).

The revelation goes on to explain the importance of faithful service and enduring to the end: "They are they who are the church of the Firstborn. They are they into whose hands the Father has given all things—they are they who are priests and kings, who have received of his fulness, and of his glory. . . . Wherefore, as it is written, they are gods, even the sons of God— wherefore, all things are theirs, whether life or death, or things present, or things to come, all are theirs and they are Christ's, and Christ is God's" (D&C 76:54–56, 58–59).

Then, speaking of living in the celestial environs of the Father, the revelation said,

> These shall dwell in the presence of God and his Christ forever and ever. These are they whom he shall bring with him, when he shall come in the clouds of heaven to reign on the earth over his people. . . . These are they who are come unto Mount Zion, and unto the city of the living God, the heavenly place, the holiest of all. These are they who have come to an innumerable company of angels, to the general assembly and church of Enoch, and of the Firstborn. . . . These are they whose bodies are celestial, whose glory is that of the sun, even the glory of God, the highest of all, whose glory the sun of the firmament is written of as being typical. (D&C 76:62–63, 66–67, 70)

President John Taylor said the following about our potential to attain the heights and exaltation of godhood through Christ: "He is capable of rising from the contracted limits of manhood to the dignity of a God, and thus through the atonement of Jesus Christ and the adoption he is capable of eternal exaltation, eternal lives and eternal progression. But this transition from his manhood to the Godhead can alone be made through a power which is superior to man—an infinite power, an eternal power, even the power of the Godhead."[138]

Chapter 17
Copernicus's Devastating Blow to Satan's Ego

"Better to reign in Hell, than to serve in Heav'n."[139]

"All is not lost; th' unconquerable will, / And study of revenge, immortal hate, / And courage never to submit or yield."[140]

Did Satan's ambition motivate him to dethrone God of his power? Why are Satan and his angles so powerful and why do they have so much influence? What are the ultimate destinies of Satan and the sons of perdition?

In the fourteenth century, Dante Alighieri crafted his epic poem *Divine Comedy*, the most well-known portion being *The Inferno*.[141] The poem depicts Dante's guided journey through hell, which consists of circles of suffering inside the earth. The inferno by inference describes sinners' suffering and rejection of their sins committed during their mortal lives.

The poem begins with Dante as narrator. He finds himself lost in a dark wood and is pursued by a lion, leopard, and she-wolf. He frantically searches for the straight way to save himself. He is aware "haunted by that fell beast, never at peace, / Who coming o'er against me, by degrees / Impell'd me where the sun in silence rests."[142] Dante is rescued by the Roman poet Virgil (a device used to instill poetic justice), and they begin a journey to hell. They come across a variety of sinners who ironically suffer fates similar to their sins.

The people Dante sees in hell are those who justified their sins while mortals and are unrepentant still. For example, a fortuneteller walks forward with his head on backward, unable to see what is ahead. The author's point is the fate of these sinners is not God inflicting revenge, justice, and punishment, but instead it is a fulfillment of the destiny the sinners have selected for themselves.

The nine circles of hell are concentric, each circle representing greater wickedness and gravity of sin, leading into the center of the earth where Satan is bound. The first and less severe circle is Limbo, where people reside who did not accept Christ. They live in a bland heaven with green fields and a castle. In the castle live the wise men and poets of the world, such as Homer, Euclid, Aristotle, and so on who were good people but were not Christian.

In the second circle of hell resides those consumed with lust in mortality. This is the first level of some punishment, where the residents are pestered by violent winds, symbolic of the lusts that carried them to and fro. Here Dante sees Cleopatra, Helen of Troy, Achilles, Paris, and others motivated by sexual love during their lifetimes.

The third circle is occupied by those guilty of gluttony. People in this circle must lie in a slushy substance that collects on the ground from a constant, putrid icy rain.

In the fourth circle are those souls afflicted by greed. Dante places both popes and cardinals in this circle, who hoarded wealth for themselves and did not use these resources to help the poor. These people are at war with each other, employing heavy weapons they must push with their chests.

In the fifth circle are the wrathful. The River Styx is depicted as black and murky, the people fight each other both on the surface and under the water.

In the sixth circle reside heretics trapped in flaming tombs. In this circle, people know of life on earth comes from seeing the future, not from observing the present. Eventually, the port of the future will be shut and it will no longer be possible for the souls suffering here to know anything at all.

In the seventh circle are people who promoted violence and suffering. A minotaur guards the entrance that leads to three circles. In the outer ring, souls are dipped into a river of boiling blood and fire. On the banks, centaurs shoot arrows into those sinners who emerge higher out of the river than they are permitted. In the middle ring are people who committed suicide and are being punished for committing acts of violence against themselves. These people are transformed into misshapen bushes and trees with gnarled thorns. In the inner ring are those violent against God (such as blashpemers) and those violent against nature (such as sodomites). Inside this circle is a desert of flaming sand. Fiery flakes rain down from the sky.

The eighth and ninth circles are those who committed fraud or treachery. To reach these circles, one must descend a steep cliff. Dante and Virgil reach the cliff by flying on the back of a Geryon, a winged monster with three heads. Dante describes the monster as having three natures: human, bestial, and reptilian. It has been explained that the Geryon is an image of fraud, having the face of an honest man on the body of a beautifully colored wyvern, with the furry paws of a lion and a poisonous sting in the scorpion-like tail.

Inside the ninth and final circle are four rings for traitors and treacherous characters from the Bible and figures from mythology. They stand on a ledge, looking down into hell. For betraying his brother, Cain is placed in ice up to his chin. Antenor of Troy, who betrayed his city to the Greeks, is placed in ice up to his chin. Ptolomaea, who invited Simon Maccabaeus and his sons to a banquet and killed them, lies in ice that covers him except for his face. Judas Iscariot, the betrayer of Christ, is completely covered in ice, with his body contorted in painful positions.

In the center of all nine concentric circles of hell is Satan. He is condemned for committing personal betrayal and treachery against God. Dante describes Satan as a terrifying winged beast with a red, black, and pale yellow face. He is waist-deep in ice, weeping tears from his six eyes and moving his six wings in an attempt to escape. The icy wind only freezes the ice harder and harder, sealing his imprisonment. From two of Satan's three faces, he chews Brutus and Cassius for assassinating Julius Caesar. And in his center mouth, Satan gnaws Judas Iscariot, with his back being forever torn by Satan's claws. Literary experts have noted that Satan is portrayed as impotent, ignorant, and full of hate, contrasted with God, who is all-powerful and all-knowing and possesses a loving nature.

Dante and Virgil escape from the lowest region of hell by climbing down Satan's matted and ragged fur, emerging before dawn on Easter Sunday under a beautiful starry sky.

I Am the God of This World

In 1543, Nicolaus Copernicus peered through his telescope to put the finishing touches on his theory of the heliocentric model of the universe.[143] Copernicus hypothesized that the sun was the center of the universe, and earth and other planets rotated around the sun in a series of circular and elliptical orbits. Copernicus's theory of a heliocentric model of the universe conflicted with the prevailing geocentric model developed by the Greeks and Ptolemy, which placed the earth at the orbital center of all celestial bodies.

Satan promotes himself as the god of this world. To the Corinthians, Paul said, "In whom the god of this world hath blinded the minds of them which believe not" (2 Corinthians 4:4).

With my reference to Copernicus, I am not suggesting that Satan promoted the Ptolemaic model that placed the earth at the center of the universe.

But I find it ironic that Satan refers to himself as the god of this world. He desires this world, where he claims to be a god, as in the center of the universe. He desires to imitate the one true God whom he attempted to dethrone and rise above in authority and power and whose residence is at the center of all His creations, which are "worlds without number" (Moses 1:33).

The scriptures teach, "Kolob is set nigh unto the throne of God, to govern all those planets which belong to the same order as that upon which thou standest" (Abraham 3:9). According to the scientists and astronomers, based on Kepler space mission data, "There could be as many as forty billion Earth-sized planets orbiting in the habitable zones of sun-like stars and red dwarf stars within the Milky Way galaxy. Eleven billion of these estimated planets may be orbiting sun-like stars. The nearest such planet may be twelve light-years away."[144]

Of Satan's ambition to strip God of His power and authority, C. S. Lewis taught,

> The moment you have a self at all, there is a possibility of putting yourself first—wanting to be the centre—wanting to be God, in fact. That was the sin of Satan: and that was the sin he taught the human race. . . . What

> Satan put into the heads of our remote ancestors was the idea that they "could be like gods"—could set up on their own as if they had created themselves—be their own masters—invent some sort of happiness for themselves outside God, apart from God. And out of that hopeless attempt has come . . . the long terrible story of man trying to find something other than God which will make him happy.[145]

Know Thy Enemy

Chinese military strategist from the second century BC Sun Tzu taught in *The Art of War* that "if you know the enemy and know yourself, you need not fear the result of a hundred battles. If you know yourself but not the enemy, for every victory gained you will also suffer a defeat. If you know neither the enemy nor yourself, you will succumb in every battle."[146]

Satan is your adversary! He is hellbent, quite literally, on sealing your fate with destruction by destroying your eternal happiness. "And because he had fallen from heaven, and had become miserable forever, he sought also the misery of all mankind" (2 Nephi 2:18). He desires to make you his.

Satan is the author of all evil in the world. Alma taught, "Whatsoever is good cometh from God, and whatsoever is evil cometh from the devil" (Alma 5:40). If Satan is the influence behind the opposition to the redemption of all of God's children, we must know how to overcome his temptations and teach others. The Apostle Paul said, "Lest Satan should get an advantage of us: for we are not ignorant of his devices" (2 Corinthians 2:11).

But if you were Father in Heaven, why permit Satan to tempt Your children? The Doctrine and Covenants gives us the answer: "And it must needs be that the devil should tempt the children of men, or they could not be agents unto themselves; for if they never should have bitter they could not know the sweet" (D&C 29:39).

In *King Lear*, Shakespeare wrote of Satan that "the prince of darkness is a gentleman."[147] In *The Merchant of Venice*, he penned the line, "The devil can cite scripture for his purpose."[148] Finally, Shakespeare wrote, "He's mad that trusts in the tameness of a wolf."[149] Just like a hungry wolf in the wild, Satan is not tame nor can he be tamed.

Nephi summed up rather nicely Satan's tactics: "And others will he pacify, and lull them away into carnal security, that they will say: All is well in Zion; yea, Zion prospereth, all is well—and thus the devil cheateth their souls, and leadeth them away carefully down to hell. And behold, others he flattereth away, and telleth them there is no hell; and he saith unto them: I am no devil, for there is none—and thus he whispereth in their ears, until he grasps them with his awful chains, from whence there is no deliverance" (2 Nephi 28:21–22).

One of the great teachings of Joseph Smith is that Satan and his angels are not all-powerful. We need not cower to Satan and his legions of tempters and temptresses if our lives are founded on heavenly light, righteousness, and life-generating powers from Heavenly Father. The Prophet taught, "All beings who have bodies have power over those who have not. The devil has no power over us only as we permit him. The moment we revolt at anything which comes from God, the devil takes power."[150] At another time, he said, "Wicked spirits have their bounds, limits, and laws, by which they are governed."[151]

Full of Wisdom and Perfect in Beauty

Is Satan the caricature we see in books and movies? Is he a red devil with a pointy tail and pitchfork, traipsing about sinisterly? Or is he one of the most beautiful angels fallen from heaven? Ezekiel wrote,

> Son of man, take up a lamentation upon the king of Tyrus [symbol for Satan], and say unto him, Thus saith the Lord God; Thou sealest up the sum, full of wisdom, and perfect in beauty. Thou hast been in Eden the garden of God; every precious stone was thy covering. . . . Thou art the anointed cherub that covereth . . . thou wast upon the holy mountain of God [celestial kingdom with us]; thou hast walked up and down in the midst of the stones of fire. Thou wast perfect in thy ways from the day that thou wast created, till iniquity was found in thee. (Ezekiel 28:12–15)

Ezekiel continued, describing Satan's beauty, "Thine heart was lifted up because of thy beauty, thou hast corrupted thy wisdom by reason of thy brightness: I will cast thee to the ground" (verse 17). Contrast Satan's "beauty" with these words from Isaiah about the Savior: "For he shall grow up before him as a tender plant, and as a root out of a dry ground:

he hath no form nor comeliness; and when we shall see him, there is no beauty that we should desire him" (Isaiah 53:2).

Yet who is the source of salvation and healing and the key to our overcoming all things that beset us? Satan may have the appearance of beauty on the outside of his personage, but inside he is full of darkness, deceit, and deviousness.

Ezekiel's comment about how Satan is "full of wisdom" should caution us that his intelligence is greater than ours. Therefore, he can easily deceive us if we allow him. Unlike us, he does not have a veil cast over his mind, concealing the memory of our former glory and stature with the Father. In many respects, he and his followers have had to watch us and learn who we really are to devise their snares. The Book of Mormon prophet Alma taught, "Because of sin and transgression, and the power of the devil, which comes by the cunning plans which he hath devised to ensnare the hearts of men" (Alma 28:13).

Many a cautionary tale can be told of people in their pride and ease of life who have succumbed to the snares of the evil one, as "he leadeth them by the neck with a flaxen cord, until he bindeth them with his strong cords forever" (2 Nephi 26:22). Therefore, we need to possess a healthy respect and caution for the powers of darkness that center in Satan and be aware of his "wisdom" and how he is "perfect in beauty."

Is This the Man Who Made the Earth to Tremble?

Isaiah spoke prophetically of Satan's fate, "How art thou fallen from heaven, O Lucifer, son of the morning! How art thou cut down to the ground. . . . Yet thou shalt be brought down to hell, to the sides of the pit. They that see thee shall narrowly look upon thee, and consider thee, saying, Is this the man that made the earth to tremble, that did shake kingdoms" (Isaiah 14:12, 15–16).

Perdition means destruction. Perdition is both a physical location and spiritual condition, just as the celestial, terrestrial, or telestial kingdoms are physical locations and spiritual conditions—and the people who inhabit these are in different resurrected states. The spiritual condition within the sons of perdition has been likened unto a lake of unquenchable fire and brimstone. The sons of perdition are "doomed to suffer the wrath of God" (D&C 76:33), or to forever experience the second death. They will experience an intense agony, like a burning from within, as they stand in God's presence to be judged as they contemplate the Father's holiness and glory in relation to their filthiness.

The Prophet Joseph Smith taught, "A man is his own tormentor and his own condemner. . . . The torment of disappointment in the mind of man is as exquisite as a lake burning with fire and brimstone."[152] If this was not horrible enough, after the sons of perdition receive the calling of their eternal damnation, they will be cast into outer darkness to be ruled over by Satan throughout eternity. Yes, "it had been better for them never to have been born" (D&C 76:32).

The Prophet also commented that he had seen in vision the fate of the sons of perdition and it was too terrible to discuss. The second death they experience is believed to be a disorganization of their physical and spiritual natures to the point that the elements of life return to "native element[s]." President Brigham Young stated, "Now understand, to choose life is to choose principles that will lead you to an eternal increase, and nothing short of them will produce life in the resurrection for the faithful. Those that choose death, make choice of the path which leads to the end of their organization. The one leads to endless increase and progression, the other to the destruction of the organized being, ending in its entire decomposition into the particles that compose the native elements."[153]

However, the ultimate destiny of sons of perdition is made known only to those who are partakers thereof. We learn in the panoramic vision of the eternal fates of all in Doctrine and Covenants Section 76: "Wherefore, he saves all except them—they shall go away into everlasting punishment, which is endless punishment, which is eternal punishment, to reign with the devil and his angels in eternity, where their worm dieth not, and the fire is not quenched, which is their torment—and the end thereof, neither the place thereof, nor their torment, no man knows" (D&C 76:44–45).

Dante's *Inferno*

Getting back to the *Inferno* mentioned at the beginning of this chapter, Dante does not mention the fate of those spirits who followed Satan in premortality. Latter-day revelation teaches that a third part of heaven followed Satan and serve as his minions, tempting us and whispering flattering, mean, and degrading things into our ears. However, their fate is similar to Satan and the sons of perdition: to be cast into outer darkness, where the life-generating powers of Father in Heaven do not reach. With no eternal light or truth to sustain their spiritual and physical bodies, they decay and drift into the darkest black conceivable.

The Doctrine and Covenants teach, "And by this you may know the righteous from the wicked, and that the whole world groaneth under sin and darkness even now" (D&C 84:53). Many people are victims of Satan and his followers. Why? They have not turned to the true and living God. The most powerful protection against spiritual death and decay is personal righteousness and heeding the Light of Christ and the Holy Ghost. They who do this will be "filled with light, and there shall be no darkness" in them (D&C 88:67). This light of heaven in the form of personal revelation provides discernment to avoid sin, transgression, mistakes, errors, and so on. It leads to keeping the commands of God.

A warning as you desire to grow spiritually and deepen your relationship with Christ: Joseph Smith taught, from personal experience, "The nearer a person approaches the Lord, a greater power will be manifested by the adversary to prevent the accomplishment of His purposes."[154]

Chapter 18
Mankind's First Estate

"They who keep their second estate shall have glory added upon their heads for ever and ever" (Abraham 3:26).

What were the purposes the three grand councils? Is there more than one plan of salvation as proposed by Lucifer? What was I foreordained to become?

The *Apocryphal Acts of the Apostles* contains a poem entitled "The Pearl."[155] The Apostle Thomas allegedly rehearsed the poem while he was in prison on his missionary travels through India. "The Pearl" is well read among LDS audiences as the symbols from the poem align nicely with concepts of heavenly parents, premorality, foreordination, heirship, and so on.

The poem is about a young man reared in his parents' glorious kingdom, where he is treated like a prince to all kinds of luxuries. His parents send him to Egypt to retrieve a special pearl for their treasury. However, a serpent guards the pearl. Before leaving on his quest, his parents remove his "glorious robe," which they promise will be restored to him if he is successful in retrieving the pearl. But as the young man travels through Egypt (a symbol for the world in many different scriptural sources), he forgets his divine heritage. "I forgot that I was a King's son, and became a slave to their king. I forgot all concerning the Pearl for which my Parents had sent me; and from the weight of their victuals I sank down into a deep sleep."[156] (Think of Adam's deep sleep in the Garden of Eden and the veil of forgetfulness.)

Apprised of their son's predicament, his parents send him a letter to awaken him to his mission and purpose in retrieving the pearl. "From Us—King of Kings, thy Father, and thy Mother, Queen of the Dawn-land. . . . Remember that thou art a King's son; see whom thou hast served in thy slavedom. . . . Remember thy Glorious Robe, thy Splendid Mantle remember, to put on and wear as adornment, when thy Name may be read in the Book of the Heroes. And with Our Successor, thy Brother, thou mayest be Heir in Our Kingdom."[157]

The letter has the desired effect. The son conquers the serpent, secures the pearl, and returns to his parents and home. He says, "I remembered that I was a King's son, and my rank did long for its nature. I bethought me again of the Pearl, for which I was sent down to Egypt. . . . Their filthy and unclean garments I stripped off and left in their country. To the way that I came I betook me, to the light of our home, to the Dawn-land. . . . In the House of my Father my childhood had left it, at once, as soon as I saw it, the Glory looked like my own self."[158]

What if we too come here, laying aside our glorious robes and confronting serpents to obtain our pearl of great worth—a redeemed and glorified resurrected body—that we may pursue eternal life in courts on high?

Our Premortal Existence

Referring to the premortal existence in his book *The Key to the Science of Theology*, Elder Parley P. Pratt taught that, as spirit children, we were reared in the immediate environs of our heavenly parents and "matured in the heavenly mansions, trained in the school of love in the family circle, and amid the most tender embraces of parental and fraternal affection."[159] Pratt also taught that we "lived and moved as a free and rational intelligence, acting upon its own agency, and, like all intelligence, independent in its own sphere."[160]

In premortality, we undoubtedly had our agency and progressed in light and truth under the direction of the Father. After all, it is Heavenly Father's desire that we become like Him to experience the joy and happiness of eternal life. Joseph Smith taught that "God . . . saw proper to institute laws whereby the rest could have a privilege to advance like himself."[161] Under the Father's loving care, in our premortal state, we were provided learning opportunities to become more like our heavenly parents. These laws that They designed help us to acquire more and more light, truth, knowledge, intelligence, power, and glory.

With our agency to obey or disobey, in some respects the type of life there was similar to this life, where we learn, experience, and grow. Explaining the type of life there, Elder Bruce R. McConkie wrote, "All the spirits of men, while yet in the Eternal Presence, developed aptitudes, talents, capacities, and abilities of every sort, kind, and degree. During the long expanse of life which then was, an infinite variety of talents and abilities came into being. As the ages rolled, no two spirits remained alike. Mozart became a musician; Einstein centered his interest in mathematics; Michelangelo turned his attention to painting. . . . Abraham and Moses and all of the prophets sought and obtained the talent for spirituality."[162]

A prevalent LDS belief is that when we pass from premortality to mortality, we bring with us certain predispositions, proclivities, and personality traits previously developed. Looking through a veil of forgetfulness in this life, we forget what happened before because we are here being tested. Elder McConkie continued, "The capacities and abilities that then were ours are yet resident within us. Mozart is still a musician; Einstein retains his mathematical abilities; Michelangelo his artistic talent; Abraham, Moses, and the prophets their spiritual talents and abilities. . . . And all men with their infinitely varied talents and personalities pick up the course of progression where they left it off when they left the heavenly realms."[163]

Councils of the Gods

There came a time when our Heavenly Father desired that His spirit children have a mortal experience, be proven on a fallen world, and continue to progress and advance in intelligence. By obedience to the laws of God, certain of His spirit children were granted permission to come to a fallen world. In a vision, Abraham was shown at least one of the three Grand Councils: "Now the Lord had shown unto me, Abraham, the intelligences that were organized before the world was; and among all these there were many of the noble and great ones. . . . Abraham, thou art one of them; thou wast chosen before thou wast born" (Abraham 3:22–23). This council consisted of hearing Lucifer's counter plan to Heavenly Father's proven plan—the only workable plan.

Joseph Smith said of the first Grand Council, "In the beginning, the head of the Gods called a council of the Gods; and they came together and concocted a plan to create the world and people it."[164] Though we were not part of the Grand Council, nor witnesses to it, we undoubtedly were aware of what occurred there on our behalf.

Relating to our premortal existence, a woman once asked Elder John Taylor the following questions: "Where did I come from? What am I doing here? Whither am I going? And what is my destiny after having obeyed the truth, if faithful to the end?" President Taylor responded,

> Knowest thou not that eternities ago, thy spirit, pure and holy, dwelt in thy Heavenly Father's bosom . . . surrounded by thy brother and sister spirits in the spirit world, among the Gods[?] That as thy spirit beheld the scenes transpiring there, and thou growing in intelligence, thou sawest worlds upon worlds organized and peopled with thy kindred spirits, [who] took upon them tabernacles, died, were resurrected, and received their exaltation on the redeemed worlds they once dwelt upon.
>
> Thou being willing and anxious to imitate them, waiting and desirous to obtain a body, a resurrection and exaltation also, and having obtained permission, thou made a covenant with one of thy kindred spirits to be thy guardian angel while in mortality. . . . Thou longed, thou sighed, and thou prayed to thy Father in heaven for the time to arrive when thou couldst come to this earth, which had fled and fell from where it was first organized.[165]

In other settings, the sons and daughters of God were taught about the Creation, the Fall, mortality, the Atonement, the resurrection, and the judgment. As the plan of salvation was revealed, our potential and anticipated mistakes from inexperience and sin were discussed. We understood that sin would lead to ultimate separation from God. But the Atonement and its infinite effects were presented to us.

Joseph F. Smith saw in a vision that we received our "first lessons in the world of spirits and were prepared to come forth in the due time of the Lord to labor in his vineyard for the salvation of the souls of men" (D&C 138:56).

Freedom of thought, expression, and action being a hallmark of exalted beings, Lucifer, a son of the morning, was permitted to offer an alternative plan to the one plan of the Gods:

> And there stood one among them that was like unto God, and he said unto those who were with him: We will go down . . . and we will make an earth. . . . And they who keep their first estate shall be added upon; and they who keep not their first estate shall not have glory in the same kingdom with those who keep their first estate; and they who keep their second estate shall have glory added upon their heads for ever and ever. . . .
>
> And the Lord said: Whom shall I send? And one answered like unto the Son of Man: Here am I, send me. And another answered and said: Here am I, send me. And the Lord said: I will send the first. And the second was angry, and kept not his first estate; and, at that day, many followed after him. (Abraham 3:24, 26, 27–28)

The "and another answered" refers to Lucifer, the son of the morning. His name also means "shining one" and "light bearer." Yes, Lucifer was part of the noble and great spirits who had progressed in righteousness, light, and truth, acquiring much of the Father's divine nature in premortality. Lucifer's plan would have negated agency. Not one soul would be lost. It was a no-risk proposition. If there were no agency, there would be no sin or transgression, and no Atonement or Savior would be necessary. But if there were no agency, there would be no growth, change, repentance, and so on. No proving process to see if we would obey the Father at all costs, so no acquiring the divine nature of our Heavenly Father.

The Prophet Joseph Smith taught, "The contention in heaven was—Jesus said there would be certain souls that would not be saved; and the devil said he could save them all, and laid his plans before the Grand Council, who gave their vote in favor of Jesus Christ."[166]

The Lord revealed to Moses more details than those in the Abraham account. Satan approached God, saying, "Behold, here am I, send me, I will be thy son, and I will redeem all mankind, that one soul shall not be lost, and surely I will do it; wherefore give me thine honor. But, behold, my Beloved Son, which was my Beloved and Chosen from the beginning, said unto me—Father, thy will be done, and the glory be thine forever." God rejected Satan's plan, and, "Satan rebelled against me, and sought to destroy the agency of man. . . . I caused that he should be cast down; and he became Satan, yea, even the devil, the father of all lies" (Moses 4:1–4).

Lucifer was essentially vying for the power of the Father and the Son. The "honor of the Father" is His power, and the Father's power was to be centered in Christ. Sufficeth to say, the son of the morning and "light bearer" and "shining one" descended in righteousness and character to become the prince of darkness. How could someone so acquainted with light and truth, and having partaken deeply of Heavenly Father's divine nature, dim and darken?

So Instead of continuing to receive truth and being nurtured with the life-generating powers of the Spirit of Truth possessed by Heavenly Father, Lucifer pridefully became an accuser of the Father, the Son, and the righteousness of the noble and great ones. "And I heard a loud voice saying in heaven, Now is come salvation . . . and the power of his Christ: for the accuser of our brethren is cast down, which accused them before our God day and night" (Revelation 12:10).

As he allowed the light that he had developed in himself through sacrifice and self-discipline to dim within himself, darkness replaced it, imprisoning Lucifer to his selfish ambitions. With the powers of goodness diminishing within, his ability to understand truth faded away also, "for he knew not the mind of God, wherefore he sought to destroy the world." (Moses 4:6).

A World Not Certain to Be Saved

Discussing dimensions of human freedom, psychologist and philosopher William James remarked,

> Suppose that the world's author put the case to you before creation, saying: "I am going to make a world not certain to be saved, a world the perfection of which shall be conditional merely, the condition being that each several agent does its own level best. I offer you the chance of taking part in such a world. Its safety, you see, is unwarranted. It is a real adventure, with real danger, yet it may win through. It is a social scheme of cooperative work genuinely to be done. Will you join the procession? Will you trust yourself and trust the other agents enough to face the risk?"[167]

James somewhat described our situation. Though an individual's salvation is yet to be determined, Heavenly Father will save all of His creations through His Only Begotten Son in a kingdom of glory fitted for their happiness. "And there is nothing that the Lord thy God shall take in his heart to do but what he will do it" (Abraham 3:17).

When Lucifer and his followers pursued their course of winning others to their side in the premortal existence, they mixed truth with error by disparaging the true plan of eternal progression. Lucifer preyed on people's individual doubts about being able to live appropriately on a fallen world, which would jeopardize their eternal progression. He distorted the elements of the one plan to cause doubt and fear. Others, however, trusted in the Father and Son's promises.

The Fundament Flaw

The fundamental flaw in Lucifer's plan is the eternal law that "all truth is independent [free] in that sphere in which God has placed it, to act for itself, as all intelligence also; otherwise there is no existence" (D&C 93:30). Put another way, the Book of Mormon teaches of the effects of the intelligent, life-generating power of positive choices: "Wherefore, men are free . . . to choose liberty and eternal life, through the great Mediator of all men, or to choose captivity and death, according to the captivity and power of the devil; for he seeketh that all men might be miserable like unto himself" (2 Nephi 2:27).

The Prophet Joseph Smith taught, "*God* would not exert any compulsory means, and the *devil* could not."[168] Under divine law, as agency is properly exercised, the intelligence in men and women increases to where they can stand independent in that truth. "For intelligence cleaveth unto intelligence; wisdom receiveth wisdom; truth embraceth truth; virtue loveth virtue; light cleaveth unto light; mercy hath compassion on mercy and claimeth her own; justice continueth its course and claimeth its own; judgment goeth before the face of him who sitteth upon the throne and governeth and executeth all things" (D&C 88:40).

As Lucifer and his followers waged their campaign in this ideological power struggle, their light, glory, and goodness dimmed in greater and greater amounts as they fought against the principles of truth and righteousness. Through their rebellion, they experienced a spiritual death, voluntarily severing the connection between Father in Heaven and the life-sustaining powers of eternal life He once willingly provided them. With the truth and light once within them now near extinct, they could not longer abide the Father's presence and were "thrust down from the presence of God and the Son" (D&C 76:25).

And the Father and all of heaven wept! They weren't glad to be rid of Satan and his followers. There was heartfelt sorrow for what they were giving up on: eternal joy, eternal families, and eternal progression. "And this we saw also, and bear record, that an angel of God who was in authority in the presence of God, who rebelled against the Only Begotten Son whom the Father loved and who was in the bosom of the Father, was thrust down from the presence of God and the Son, and was called Perdition, for the heavens wept over him—he was Lucifer, a son of the morning. And we beheld, and lo, he is fallen! Is fallen, even a son of the morning!" (D&C 76:25–27).

Despite being cast out of heaven, Lucifer remains a powerful force. Joseph Smith explained, "Think of a spirit who was sufficiently courageous to measure strength with his Father and Elder Brother, defying their authority! And when cast from heaven for his rebellion could have a retinue of one third of its innumerable hosts to follow him . . . his influence can only be rebuked by the great Jehovah, who restrains his power only when attempting a greater destruction than was allowed his majesty."[169]

Conclusion: The Veil of Forgetfulness

We read of these premortal events with no memory of them ourselves. But what if there were no veil of forgetfulness? The shock of entering this world from our former celestial home, degrading to a lower telestial world, would be a dark experience, both physically and psychologically. If that life-giving light that previously warmed and sustained us were immediately withdrawn, we would find ourselves in a state of despair and depression. But instead, we come into this world barely conscious of ourselves.

A newborn infant squints into the light of the world, forming neural pathways through the brain. An infant psychologically cannot distinguish himself or herself from the mother who holds and nurtures him or her.

Then the slow unfolding process of individuality begins as we rediscover gradually who we really are, which occurs over a lifetime. Do we ever fully rediscover who we are in this life? Or will we have to wait until the resurrection when eons of our premortal memories are restored to see ourselves for who we really are and have become?

Elder B. H. Roberts said, "Faith is simply trust in what the spirit learned eons ago."[170] The Doctrine and Covenants teach, "Man is spirit" (D&C 93:33). We also learn from those inspired revelations that if we do not receive the Spirit, we are "under condemnation" (D&C 93:32). But if we receive the light, it will grow "brighter and brighter until the perfect day" (D&C 50:24). And "the Spirit giveth light to every man that cometh into the world; and the Spirit enlighteneth every man through the world, that hearkeneth to the voice of the Spirit" (D&C 84:46).

President Lorenzo Snow said, "We were selected, ordained, and set apart there according to our worthiness and preparation and training to come forth when our preparation fitted clearly into the great plan of our Father. And as we live worthy the Holy Spirit brings this knowledge to this body, and that is the only way we become acquainted with the knowledge of our spiritual understanding. This body must get acquainted with former pre-existent experiences through being revealed to, and made a part of, this flesh."[171]

To rediscover who we were as eternally existing sons and daughters of God, we must move in the direction of spiritual insights and intuitions. If we are part of the Church and kingdom of God, it is clear where our allegiances lay in premortality.

Chapter 19
Trailing Clouds of Glory from Premortality

"Everything in our life happens as though we entered upon it with a load of obligations contracted in a previous existence . . . obligations whose sanction is not of this present life, [which] seem to belong to a different world, founded on kindness, scruples, sacrifice, a world entirely different from this one, a world whence we emerge to be born on this earth, before returning thither."[172]

Is there more to me, and what is in my mind, than can be accounted for by experiences in this life? Did I foreknow the trials and tribulations of this life and still shout for joy?

In a slight twist on a parable, a man travels to a faraway city. He falls among thieves, is robbed of his money and goods, suffers a head injury in the attack, and is left with amnesia. He does not remember who he is and where he came from or his home and family, and therefore has no desire or knowledge to return, though family and friends are anxious that he return to them. But as time passes, shadowy vestiges of memories return, leaving him wondering if "[he's] a stranger here, / And [he] felt that [he] had wandered from a more exalted sphere," to borrow a phrase from Eliza R. Snow.[173]

Poets visualize things in symbols and metaphor. They bring insights and truths not discoverable through logic. Contemplating the depths of human consciousness, poet William Blake was convinced that his mind was filled with "books and pictures of old, which [he] wrote and painted in ages of eternity before [his] mortal life."[174] Thomas Traherne's poem "The Salutation" suggests that this world is a gift from Father in Heaven for His children to come visit: "Long time before, / I in my mother's womb was born, / A God preparing did this glorious store / The world for me adorn. / Into the Eden so divine and fair / So wide and bright, I come His son and heir."[175]

Life invokes the imagery of actors in a three-act play, though with a somewhat undefined, improvisational script. Elder Neal A. Maxwell, a prophet and seer who understood the purposes of premortality, taught, "Fortunately, the veil keeps the first, second, and third estates separate—hence our sense of separateness. The veil avoids having things "compound in one" to our everlasting detriment (2 Nephi 2:11). We are cocooned, as it were, in order that we might truly choose. Once, long ago, we chose to come to this very setting where we could choose. It was an irrevocable choice. And the veil is the guarantor that our ancient choice will be honored."[176]

What experiences, memories, and intelligence are locked under the amnesia of your veil of forgetfulness—the spiritual film that wears thin at times, revealing shadows of our former selves and the worlds we once knew?

Déjà Vu and Our "Depth" Selves

Déjà vu is a French word meaning "already seen." The experience is characterized by a strong feeling that you have experienced an event previously and that you are "reliving" it. To account for the depth in people that cannot be easily explained by life experiences, some turn to the idea of reincarnation or the transmigration of souls, or experiences and knowledge gleaned from other previous lives. But could premortal existence be the explanation? There is something that lies below our sense of self. Could this be who we became premortally, through pre-earthly opportunities and endowments of the Father?

Depth psychology is a social science that explores the relationship between consciousness and unconsciousness in our mental states, the depths within us that lie below the surface. Psychologist and philosopher William James commented that there may exist a reservoir of spiritual insight that we can break into and recognize.[177]

Could this reservoir of myth and images for humanity come from actual experiences in our premortal existence? President Joseph F. Smith observed how "we often catch a spark from the awakened memories of the immortal soul, which lights up our whole being as with the glory of our former home."[178] Elder Neal A. Maxwell said, "There can be sudden surges of *déjà vu.* A flash from the mirror of memory can beckon us forward to that far pavilion, filled with 'everlasting splendours' and resurrected beings."[179]

"Man Is Spirit"

A fundamental teaching of the Church is that there is an eternity of intelligent matter, that matter and intelligence are eternal and have always existed. We also learn that intelligent matter possesses an affinity for like matter and form organized units of greater and greater intelligence. According to Orson Pratt, these intelligences constitute, among other things, an innumerable host of uncreated persons.[180]

In Doctrine and Covenants 93, we learn that intelligences acts freely and are independent in the sphere that God places them. Intelligences are predisposed to obey God, but there is no compulsion to do so. God, over vast amounts of time, has acquired the ability to command the intelligences, and they freely obey. The light "proceedeth forth from the presence of God to fill the immensity of space" and gives life to all things (D&C 88:12). It is the law by which "all things are governed, even the power of God who sitteth upon his throne" (verse 13).

According to philosopher Dr. Garland E. Tickemyer,

> Mormon doctrine holds that these self-moving particles of intelligences have united and through eons of time have evolved into two glorious personages whose substance, knowledge, wisdom, and goodness, though eternal, at the same time represent the highest point of development in an ever-ascending scale of being.
>
> The all-powerful substance out of which God himself evolved possesses the potential for development of myriad personal spirits of like character and ultimate power. This, in fact, explains the origin and nature of man. The Prophet's statement is that "man was also in the beginning with God. . . . Intelligence . . . was not created." [Elder] Orson Pratt's position appears to be that out of pre-existing eternal matter God formed spiritual bodies and implanted within them a pre-existent divine spark. He shoved those bits of incarnate intelligence on their way, and the fact

> of their primal independence of all other intelligence accounts for their inherent freedom of will. Pratt held that God did not create intelligent beings; he formed them, and he has limited control over them.[181]

Referring to our time as intelligences, Doctrine and Covenants 93 states, "Man was also in the beginning with God. Intelligence, or the light of truth, was not created or made, neither indeed can be" (D&C 93:29). Commenting on this doctrine, Joseph Smith said, "The intelligence of spirits had no beginning, neither will it have an end."[182]

The Prophet also taught that intelligences are at various stages of development. If given the opportunity by God, they may become His spirit children and go on to acquire a physical body and attain, by their choices, a degree of glory and perfection. "God himself, finding he was in the midst of spirits and glory, because he was more intelligent, saw proper to institute laws whereby the rest could have a privilege to advance like himself."[183]

Therefore, God coexists with individualized intelligences who are conscious and have the freedom to act, develop personality and identity, and respond to the light that "proceedeth forth from the presence of God to fill the immensity of space" (D&C 88:12). Simply put, God's work and glory is to love, motivate, and encourage the intelligent constituent parts of the universe to advance to higher states of glory and existence and experience joy.

Elder B. H. Robert taught, "To this Supreme Intelligence [God] are the other Intelligences necessary. He without them cannot be perfect, nor they without Him. There is community of interest between them; also of love and brotherhood; and hence community of effort for the mutual good, for progress, for attainment of the highest possible. Therefore are these Eternal Divine Intelligences drawn together in oneness of mind and purpose—in moral and spiritual unity."[184]

Formation of Spirit Bodies with Intelligence and Ego

Premortally, at some point in development, the primal intelligences were conjoined with other spiritual elements to form spirit bodies. These spirit bodies were conceived by our heavenly parents. In 1839, Joseph Smith told Zina Diantha Huntington after the death of her mother that "not only would she know her mother again on the other side, but 'more than that, you will meet and become acquainted with your eternal Mother.' . . . To which she uttered in amazement and wonder, 'And have I then a Mother in Heaven?' 'You assuredly have,' Joseph answered. 'How could a Father claim His title unless there were also a Mother to share that parenthood?' "[185]

President Spencer W. Kimball taught, "The Primary song says, 'I am a child of God.' Born with a noble birthright. God is your father. He loves you. He and your mother in heaven value you beyond any measure. They gave your eternal intelligence spirit form, just as your earthly mother and father have given you a mortal body. You are unique. One of a kind, made of the eternal intelligence which gives you claim upon eternal life."[186]

Through spirit birth, we literally become the offspring of deity. The Apostle Paul said, "Forasmuch then as we are the offspring of God" (Acts 17:29). This is not just the formation or organization of a physical tabernacle from spiritual and intelligent matter. Through conception, divine characteristics are instilled within. Put poetically, President John Taylor taught that we come from "a spark of Deity, struck from the fire of his eternal blaze, and brought forth in the midst of eternal burnings."[187]

Conclusion

Knowing of our premortal existence, people do not need to wonder over the question, Is life purposeful? Life is not an absurd collection of contradictions that we must endure. We come here for a reason. Our intelligence, or the Light of Truth, is eternal and has always existed. We lived as spirit children of God in a premortal existence, and God is the Father of the spirits of all mankind. Our instruction and preparation for earth life began in the world of spirits, and God gave us agency there. He provided the plan of salvation by which His spirit children could eventually become like Him.

Chapter 20
The Purposeful Fall

"So hand in hand they passed, the loveliest pair that ever since in love's embraces met—Adam the goodliest man of men since born his sons; the fairest of her daughters Eve."[188]

How was the Fall purposeful and good for me? Is original sin a myth? Was man really conceived in sin?

In the novel *The Garden Gate*,[189] the character Summer Walker has a dream.

> In the dream, the orchard was in early morning. Summer placed her hand against a tree and peered down a row of trees.
>
> "Come closer."
>
> Summer walked down a row of trees in her bare feet and stood by a tree in a beautiful garden. A slender-faced man approached her, his cane craved in twists with a snakehead for a handle.
>
> "You have a beautiful garden here," complimented the man pleasantly.
>
> "Yes. It is beautiful."
>
> "Please walk with me?" he smiled gentlemanly pointing down the row with his cane.
>
> Summer walked by the side of the man. He said pleasant, flattering things to her. The man looked out over the river. A band of light rose above the southeastern horizon. The sky was blue and thin trails of clouds scattered across it.

"Surely you can eat of the fruit of this beautiful garden? It would be a shame to create such a beautiful place and not be able to partake," said the man.

"Yes, we may eat of the fruit of the trees of the garden—of all but one."

"All but one? What if you partake of this one fruit?"

"I must leave this beautiful garden."

"Can you leave this garden without partaking of this fruit?"

"No. I must partake if I'm ever to leave."

"Oh my, what a pity. A prisoner in a beautiful garden. There are worse fates I would guess," gently laughed the man. "Do you know what is outside this garden?"

"No. Do you?"

"Why, yes. I've been to many gardens like this and other gardens even more grand. Do you ever wonder what it is like outside of your prison garden here?"

"I do."

"Well, my dear, there are gardens immensely more beautiful outside this garden. Would you like to go there with me?"

"I would," answered Summer innocently.

"To be all-wise, all-knowing, you need to leave this garden."

"Is that true?"

"Show me to this tree with fruit you cannot partake of."

Summer and the man walked to a towering tree in the center of the garden with low-hanging fruit. The man plucked a piece of its fruit, raising it to his face. He breathed in its aroma and hefted it in his hand.

"Here, take this. Hold it," he said handing the fruit to Summer, clasping her fingers around it.

"I was told not to touch it."

"You are touching it now and there is no harm."

Summer looked at the fruit in her hand.

"Summer. Yes, this is a beautiful garden. But there are even more beautiful gardens, gardens even more fair than you. Partake of this fruit and go there with me. You must become all-wise, all-knowing."

In the dream, Summer took the fruit and bit through the skin. She looked up at the man and his now sinister grin. Summer's eyes dropped to the garden floor.

"Out of curiosity, what does it taste like?" asked the man with mouth-watering anticipation.

"Bittersweet," said Summer. "Here, see for yourself," said Summer, extending the fruit to him.

"No, no," said the old gentleman waving his hand at the fruit in fear and disgust.

The Fall Forward into the Eastern Morning Light

The sun rises in the east. As morning light edges over the horizon, nature responds to the promise of a new day. With the first rays of morning light—based on the wavelength of sunlight received—the physiology and behavior of plants and animals change. Environmental sensors connected to nerve systems produce chemical reactions to the sunlight, with flowers and fauna blossoming and changing color. Trees absorb the sunlight, blocking light so that it does not reach some of the plant life below. Possessing a natural desire to be nourished by sunlight, seedlings that are unable to feed on the sun's rays shift their energy into elongation, not leafing out but growing and stretching to reach the sunlight.

The placement of the Garden of Eden "eastward in Eden" (Moses 3:8) was purposeful—a teaching device for Adam and Eve and us. The garden was placed in a position to receive the first rays of the morning light coming from the east, symbolic of the light and knowledge that descends from heaven to earth. Also, when Adam and Eve left the garden, they traveled eastward, moving further in the direction of more light and knowledge.

Misunderstanding of the Fall and Original Sin

To understand the context of our mortal experience—where we bring with us our eternal yet unfinished selves and divine potential inherited from heavenly parents—we need to understand the truth behind the purposeful Fall.

Children do not come into this world tainted with sin of any kind. They are pure, good, and innocent. "But little children are alive in Christ, even from the foundation of the world" (Moroni 8:12). "God having redeemed man from the fall, men became again, in their infant state, innocent before God" (D&C 93:38). Children naturally possess Christlike characteristics of love and kindness. The celestial elements of which they are made have not rubbed off from contact with this telestial world.

Like Pandora lifting the lid on the jar that contained all the evils in the world, Adam and Eve have been mistakenly blamed for the ills of human nature and the harsh conditions of this mortal world. Elder Dallin H. Oaks said, "Some Christians condemn Eve for her act, concluding that she and her daughters are somehow flawed by it. Not the Latter-day Saints! Informed by revelation, we celebrate Eve's act and honor her wisdom and courage in the great episode called the Fall. Joseph Smith taught that it was not a 'sin,' because God had decreed it."[190]

However, the Garden of Eden was intended as a temporary abode. It was not to be the home for all humanity, living blissfully and innocently among the beautiful flowers throughout eternity. It is also believed by many religions that because of our first parents' choice, mankind has suffered a nearly insurmountable separation from God. Because of mankind's fallen nature, not everyone has the will to repent and show the self-discipline to follow Christ, so men and women end up piling sin upon sin through their sinful natures, becoming lost forever.

LDS Church theology firmly counters a belief in original sin. To indicate the importance of this teaching, the Articles of Faith state, "We believe that men will be punished for their own sins, and not for Adam's transgression" (Articles of Faith 1:2). Stressing the importance of this belief, it ranks second to the statement, "We believe in God, the Eternal Father, and in His Son, Jesus Christ, and in the Holy Ghost" (Articles of Faith 1:1).

However, one of the great messages of the restored gospel is that the Fall was intentional on our part. We shouted for joy at the prospects of coming to this fallen world to learn to be more like Heavenly Father, in light, truth, happiness, and creative powers. Eve's decision to eat the fruit of the tree of knowledge of good and evil meant that she would be making a sacrifice for a much better reward—an eternal reward of being more like our heavenly parents and receiving the blessings of eternal life. She, along with Adam, selflessly relinquished her paradisiacal garden of ease and comfort, perpetuated by the terrestrial rays of light from our Father in Heaven's presence. They chose to walk into the heat of a thorny, thistle-ridden telestial world of sweaty work, where one day they would experience death. "Thou shalt return unto the ground—for thou shalt surely die" (Moses 4:25).

Eve is the true hero in this story! We are eternally indebted to her for her brave choice. She nicely summed up the whole of mortal life, saying, "Were it not for our transgression we never should have had seed, and never should have known good and evil, and the joy of our redemption, and the eternal life which God giveth unto all the obedient" (Moses 5:11).

The Fall was intentional and no surprise to Heavenly Father. It was a necessary step in the progression of the human family. Foreknowing sin, mistakes, transgressions, and so on, and that His children would grow and learn to overcome sin to become more like the Father, a Savior was provided as the plan was presented, even in premortality before the creation of the earth.

Therefore, Adam and Eve acted on our behalf and made a choice to usher in mortality. The Prophet Joseph Smith taught that Adam was foreordained to "open the ways the world"[191] and begin peopling the earth with Eve.

Leaving Eden, looking over their shoulders, they could see cherubim, angels of light and glory, guarding "the way of the tree of life" (Moses 4:31). If they were to turn back and partake of the fruit of that tree, it would have counteracted the forces of death and deterioration that they had introduced into their bodies and lived forever, but in their now fallen state.

They needed to move forward. They could not go back and partake and live forever in their sins. That would have meant living without eternal progression for them or us. Looking forward, they could see a new world fraught with opportunities to be tried and tested and gain experiences they could not have otherwise experienced in their former heavenly paradise. The fiery swords of the cherubim urged them forward to the Savior and His Atonement. Therefore, they ventured forth, looking ahead into the easterly rising sun of soul-making, life-enhancing experiences.

A Handful of Dust and a Rib

In their terrestrial state before the Fall, Adam and Eve could not die, nor experience good and evil through a mortal body. Death had not entered the world. However, after the Fall, their flesh became mortal and subject to death. Therefore, the reference to man being formed from the dust of the ground is saying metaphorically that after the Fall, Adam and Eve's bodies would die. Buried in the earth—with no living system quickened by their spiritual bodies—their mortal bodies would eventually decay.

Only in their fallen condition could they learn certain things. The prophet Lehi taught, "Wherefore they would have remained in a state of innocence, having no joy, for they knew no misery; doing no good, for they knew no sin" (2 Nephi 2:23).

As stated earlier, Eve said, unequivocal after receiving a revelation, "Were it not for our transgression we never should have had seed, and never should have known good and evil, and the joy of our redemption, and the eternal life which God giveth unto all the obedient" (Moses 5:11). In this telestial world, they could experience the contrasts and dissimilarities of good and evil in ways they previously could not. They learned of opposites and the positive and negative forms of good and evil, pleasure and pain, sickness and health, virtue and vice, and so on.

This world is one of opposites, where we feel consequences in our bodies and minds, the good tending toward eternal life and evil toward sin and the death of our divine attributes. This real schooling experience was intended to be a relatively brief mortal experience, contrasted to our seeming timelessness spent in premortality. But as the restored gospel states, once we have acquired this experience and knowledge that the Father possesses—"become as one of us [Gods] to know good and evil" (Moses 4:28)—we would then be redeemed from our fallen state by our obedience and faithfulness. We can then use this "intelligence," or knowledge of good and evil, to bless ourselves, our families, and countless others for time and all eternity. Therefore, passing through this fallen, mortal state is essential to the Father's plan of ensuring the immortality and eternal life of His children.

In the Presence of God

In the garden, the Father walked and talked with Adam and Eve and "intelligence burst upon his [Adam and Eve's] understanding."[192] The Father's glory and power transformed them both, as well as all life and vegetation in the Garden of Eden. The Prophet Joseph Smith described God's glory as, "When the light rested upon me I saw two Personages, whose brightness and glory defy all description" (Joseph Smith—History

1:17). In Orson Pratt's retelling of Joseph's First Vision, he said that Joseph "saw a pillar of light brighter than the noonday sun that slowly descended on him, growing in brightness as it descended and lighting the entire area for some distance. As the light reached the tree tops, Smith feared the trees might catch fire. But when it reached the ground and enveloped him, it produced a 'peculiar sensation.' His mind was caught away from the natural objects with which he was surrounded; and he was enwrapped in a heavenly vision."[193]

Can you imagine walking and talking with God for extended periods of time, as Adam and Eve did? Try to picture being enwrapped in the heavenly glory of the Father, with intelligent, warm, life-generating light radiating through and around your corporeal being. From the second *Lectures on Faith*, we learn that "after man was created, he was not left without intelligence, or understanding, to wander in darkness, and spend an existence in ignorance and doubt. . . . God conversed with him face to face: in his presence he was permitted to stand, and from his own mouth he was permitted to receive instruction—he heard his voice, walked before him, and gazed upon his glory—while intelligence burst upon his understanding, and enabled him to give names to the vast assemblage of his Maker's works."[194]

Left alone in the garden, Eve and Adam partook of the fruit. "The serpent beguiled me, and I did eat," said Eve later, explaining her actions (Genesis 3:13). It's a great love story, Eve's sacrifice for us, and Adam following her into mortality to honor the Father in "bring[ing] to pass the immortality and eternal life of man" (Moses 1:39).

The Book of Mormon prophet Alma taught, "Our first parents were cut off both temporally and spiritually from the presence of the Lord" (Alma 42:7). God's glory withdrew, sinking the earth into its current telestial state of relative darkness, the main light coming from the sun as it receives light and power through Christ. The Garden of Eden and the rest of the world were no longer in a paradisiacal state.

The withdrawal of God's glory from the earth and our first parents is known as the first spiritual death. Perhaps it is called a spiritual death because a portion of God's glory, His rejuvenating and life-giving powers, have been withdrawn from the earth.

Alma taught that Adam being cast out of God's presence "brought upon all mankind a spiritual death" (Alma 42:9). The Lord revealed to the Prophet Joseph Smith, "Wherefore, I, the Lord God, caused that he should be cast out from the Garden of Eden, from my presence, because of his transgression, wherein he became spiritually dead, which is the first death, even that same death which is the last death, which is spiritual, which shall be pronounced upon the wicked when I shall say: Depart, ye cursed" (D&C 29:41).

Chapter 21
Redemption from the Fall

"After man was created, he was not left without intelligence, or understanding, to wander in darkness, and spend an existence in ignorance and doubt. . . . God conversed with him face to face . . . while intelligence burst upon his understanding."[195]

Why did mankind need to fall? How is Christ my hope of redemption? Can Christ really restore me from my lost and fallen condition?

In the work *The Forgotten Books of Eden*, there is what is considered the earliest prophecy of the coming of Christ:

> Then Adam said unto God: "O Lord, take Thou my soul, and let me not see this gloom any more; or remove me to some place where there is no darkness." But God the Lord said to Adam, "Verily I say unto thee, this darkness will pass from thee, every day I have determined for thee, until the fulfilment of My covenant; when I will save thee and bring thee back again into the garden, into the abode of light thou longest for, wherein is no darkness. I will bring thee, to it—in the kingdom of heaven."[196]

In another section of *The Forgotten Books of Eden*, Adam is told,

> "O Adam, as to the fruit of the Tree of Life, for which thou askest, I will not give it thee now, but when the 5500 years are fulfilled. Then will

> I give thee of the fruit of the Tree of Life, and thou shalt eat, and live for ever, thou, and Eve, and thy righteous seed. But these forty-three days cannot make amends for the hour in which thou didst transgress My commandment. O Adam, I gave thee to eat of the fig-tree in which thou didst hide thyself. Go and eat of it, thou and Eve. I will not deny thy request, neither will I disappoint thy hope; therefore, bear up unto the fulfilment of the covenant I made with thee." And God withdrew His Word from Adam.[197]

These apocryphal accounts beg the question, Why did man need to fall to be brought "back again into the garden, into the abode of light thou longest for, wherein is no darkness"? The scriptures allude, for mankind, to a brilliant future of light and truth in eternal realms after passing through this veil of tears in a world of opposites. This is all made possible by the promise of a Savior.

The Lord Reveals the Plan of Redemption

After being cast out of their garden paradise, Adam and Eve "began to till the earth, and to have dominion over all the beasts of the field, and to eat his bread by the sweat of his brow" (Moses 5:1). Adam and Eve began a family, as they had been commanded to multiply and replenish the earth.

Adam and Eve did not lose their memories of life in the Garden of Eden and their interactions with Heavenly Father. Longing to return to the glory-filled presence of the Father, they prayed and heard "the voice of the Lord from the way toward the Garden of Eden, speaking unto them, and they saw him not; for they were shut out from his presence" (Moses 5:4).

They were commanded to worship the Lord and offer the firstlings of their flocks to Him. We know that "Adam was obedient unto the commandments of the Lord" (verse 5). Then we are told that "after many days" an angel appeared to Adam and asked, "Why dost thou offer sacrifices unto the Lord?" Adam answered, "I know not, save the Lord commanded me" (verse 6).

The angel declared, "This thing is a similitude of the sacrifice of the Only Begotten of the Father, which is full of grace and truth. Wherefore, thou shalt do all that thou doest in the name of the Son, and thou shalt repent and call upon God in the name of the Son forevermore" (verses 7–8).

Adam then said, "Blessed be the name of God, for because of my transgression my eyes are opened, and in this life I shall have joy, and again in the flesh I shall see God" (verse 10).

Eve added to this with gladness, "Were it not for our transgression we never should have had seed, and never should have known good and evil, and the joy of our redemption, and the eternal life which God giveth unto all the obedient" (verse 11).

The text says that Adam and Eve blessed the name of God and taught the gospel to their sons and daughters. Then Satan made an appearance, saying, "I am also a son of God; and he commanded them, saying: Believe it not; and they believed it not, and they loved Satan more than God. And men began from that time forth to be carnal, sensual, and devilish" (verse 13).

In passing, let me add that most people associate human tendencies toward carnality, sensuality, and devilishness with a fallen nature. However, those characteristics are choices that we make and allow to develop within ourselves. The fallen nature of Adam and Eve encompassed goodness and compassion and integrity.

The Atonement Sustains Us as Fallen Mortals

Though fallen, the world is not lost. The Atonement was in effect prior to and immediately after Adam and Eve stepped out of the garden into the telestial world. Christ, speaking of Himself, declared, "I am the true light that lighteth every man that cometh into the world" (D&C 93:2). Adam and Eve, and all of us, are sustained day to day by the powers of the Atonement of Christ. Just think of it! The powers of the Atonement were operational even before Christ victoriously completed it in actuality.

King Benjamin from the Book of Mormon taught his people about humankind's dependence on Christ in this fallen world: "I say unto you, my brethren, that if you should render all the thanks and praise which your whole soul has power to possess, to that God who has created you, and has kept and preserved you, and has caused that ye should rejoice . . . and is preserving you from day to day, by lending you breath, that ye may live and move and do according to your own will, and even supporting you from one moment to another" (Mosiah 2:20–21).

King Benjamin continued, "And now, in the first place, he hath created you, and granted unto you your lives, for which ye are indebted unto him. And secondly, he doth require that ye should do as he hath commanded you; for which if ye do, he doth immediately bless you; and therefore he hath paid you. . . . Ye cannot say that ye are even as much as the dust of the earth; yet ye were created of the dust of the earth; but behold, it belongeth to him who created you" (Mosiah 2:23–25).

Suspended between Light and Perdition

In this mortal life, we are suspended, as it were, between glory and perdition—glory being that which is of God and perdition being that which is of the damned. We are given agency to see what we will choose. According to the Doctrine and Covenants 101, "That every man may act in doctrine and principle pertaining to futurity, according to the moral agency which I have given unto him, that every man may be accountable for his own sins in the day of judgment" (D&C 101:78).

Lehi taught his sons, "Wherefore, men are free according to the flesh; and all things are given them which are expedient unto man. And they are free to choose liberty and eternal life, through the great Mediator of all men, or to choose captivity and death, according to the captivity and power of the devil; for he seeketh that all men might be miserable like unto himself" (2 Nephi 2:27).

Then Lehi gives his sons this encouragement: "And now, my sons, I would that ye should look to the great Mediator . . . and choose eternal life, according to the will of his Holy Spirit; and not choose eternal death, according to the will of the flesh and the evil which is therein, which giveth the spirit of the devil power to captivate, to bring you down to hell, that he may reign over you in his own kingdom" (2 Nephi 2:28–29).

Mankind Conceived in Sin, but Not Born in Sin

The Apostle Paul, speaking of resurrection, made the following points about our mortal bodies, that we are "sown in corruption; it is raised in incorruption: it is sown in dishonour; it is raised in glory: it is sown in weakness; it is raised in power" (1 Corinthians 15:42–43).

We make our entrance into the world already in a fallen state. Adam was told, "Inasmuch as thy children are conceived in sin, even so when they begin to grow up, sin conceiveth in their hearts, and they taste the bitter, that they may know to prize the good" (Moses 6:55).

Through our conception, the fusion of two gamete cells that initiate the development of a new human, the predisposition of human frailty and a future death are implanted into the embryo. Being "conceived in sin" refers to mortal corruption sown into the body, which if adhered to leads to selfishness, pride, animosity, hatred, greed, lust, gluttony, and more.

An important teaching in Church doctrine is that at conception we receive our fallen natures, not at birth. Children are born into this world pure and innocent because of the Atonement of Christ, though they are beings with dual natures.

As fallen mortals, when children pass the age of accountability, they surrender to some degree to the mortal elements of corruption inherent in us. As innocent spirits, children have the capacity to receive light and truth to overcome the corrupt and fallen predispositions in their natures.

King Benjamin taught similarly, "For the natural man is an enemy to God, and has been from the fall of Adam, and will be, forever and ever, unless he yields to the enticings of the Holy Spirit" (Mosiah 3:19).

"Natural man" refers to our innate fallen natures. This predisposition to yield to the elements of corruption of our physical bodies will remain until we desire to reach up to God, at which point the Holy Spirit will cause an even greater change of heart.

Then as we exercise more faith and engage in good works, "it is like a grain of mustard seed, which a man took, and cast into his garden; and it grew, and waxed a great tree; and the fowls of the air lodged in the branches of it" (Luke 13:19)—Joseph Smith taught that the fowls are a symbol for angels that attend men and women who reach a certain point of righteousness.

When we experience a "mighty change of heart," the Holy Spirit enters our lives, and we are edified and uplifted and feel a newness of life. We desire to be like Christ. We receive spiritual strength to put off the natural man. We lose our desires for sin and temptations lose their effectiveness. "We are made alive in Christ because of our faith" (2 Nephi 25:25).

Christ allows us to receive light and truth and change through a sanctification process. "And again, if ye by the grace of God are perfect in Christ, and deny not his power, then are ye sanctified in Christ by the grace of God" (Moroni 10:33).

Conclusion

The power of the Atonement puts an end to every negative consequence of Adam and Eve's transgression, and we can progress beyond Adam and Eve's naïve innocence in the garden.

Through the Father's graciousness, we will receive a glorified resurrected physical body and an experiential knowledge of good and evil. If we become new creatures in Christ, possessing divine natures, we become like Christ.

The only way that mankind learns in soul-building ways is by being free. Through freedom, we learn by experience to prize the good over the evil, discern between truth and error, and love endlessly as the Savior loves us—because that is the highest form of happiness.

Adam and Eve acquired light and knowledge in this mortal sphere that they could gain in no other way. Elder Bruce C. Hafen taught, "Their years of mortal experience with repentance, humility, sorrow, and faithful striving became the Lord's course of instruction to help Adam and Eve developed the capacity to live a meaningful celestial life."[198]

We follow in the footsteps of Adam and Eve out of the Garden of Eden. There are no backdoors or shortcuts to the celestial kingdom and God's presence—only gates of circling flames we must be worthy to pass through.

We must first pass through the Edenic innocence of childhood and into the lone and dreary world of adolescence and adulthood. Then we have to pass through the portal of death and into a spirit paradise or prison.

There, we prepare further to stand in the presence of the Father to be judged. Our worthiness will shine in the brightness of our future redeemed state, with the shining radiance and brilliance of a celestial nature, the moonlit terrestrial shining countenance, or the lesser light of a faraway telestial star.

Chapter 22
Death and Other Glances over Our Shoulders at Life

"This is the terror; to have emerged from nothing, to have a name, consciousness of self, deep inner feelings, an excruciating inner yearning for life, and self-expression—and with all this yet to die. It seems like a hoax."[199]

What is the purpose of life? What is the mystery of my being? What is my pearl of great worth? Can I become perfect? How will Christ transform my mortal nature into His divine nature?

The old farmer, with his broken-down body, knew he wouldn't last much longer. He sat in his chair looking, out the large family room window into the open yard. He watched the swing that he had tied to the towering maple tree as a younger man. The swing moved in the wind, as if one of his children were on it, swinging lazily on a summer day.

The old farmer listened to his wife clanking around in the kitchen. Looking beyond the tree and swing in the front yard, he surveyed the fields where he had herded sheep and cows and raised corn and barley crops, remembering the good and bad years. He remembered his younger self, happy and joy-filled, standing in the fields, looking out across the freshly plowed and overturned earth, and then out to the river and up at the fall sky with the trails of cumulus clouds and the mountains on the horizons, where he would ride his horses. That day as a younger man, he felt alone, the only sounds coming from the wind that glided speedily over the fields.

Coming back to the present, he thought of dying soon and leaving the farm and his wife—who he had spent most of his life with because they married young—his children who were so dear to him, and his precious grandchildren. He thought of his years spent toiling to milk the cows, mend the fences, clean out ditches, and more. He loved the farm. He loved his family.

Through the walls of the old farmhouse he could hear the porch door open and his daughter coming inside. "How are you feeling today, Daddy?"

"Parts of me are just fine."

"Oh, Dad," she sighed, cocking her head in the way he remembered her.

"I'm ready for the next step," he said, pointing heavenward.

"Pain any better?"

The old farmer did not answer. He looked away from her and out into the yard at the swing moving in the wind and imagined his daughter younger swinging and laughing there, his old blue eyes watering a bit.

"I'd like to see the fields and the town," he said.

"Can you make it to the car?"

"To see the fields and town, I can," he said, smiling.

With the help of his wife and daughter, the old farmer fitted himself into the front seat of the car. Pulling away from the house, the car bounced in the rutted dirt roads that hemmed in the fields. Looking through the barbed wire past the irrigation ditches, he watched the acreage. It was a cold December day, but the sky was clear and pale. In town, he asked to drive by Jesse Sterling's house and the Bastian home, where he home taught for years. He loved that family. He asked to drive past June Crowther's old home and see what Clift had done to it, Travis Blackburn's barn to see his fruit trees, and then down to Christensen's ranch. His head turned to the window, watching the passing scenery—the things he had known and felt all his life—whiz pass him again.

The realization that this would be the last time her father would see these things he loved so much choked his daughter with emotion. She thought of the true greatness of the man, not worldly-wise in a controlling or manipulating way, but rather filled with good common sense and wisdom. She remembered her cousins coming to work the farm in the summer months because they loved Uncle Rex. He was so much fun to be around. She remembered him singing "Yellow Bird" and other songs while he worked. And the most tender memory of all, coming around the corner and seeing her father teaching a handicapped boy how to tie his shoes or tell time. The boy would come to the farm to be with her father, and her father never sent him away.

If our purpose is to come to earth to become more like the Father and the Son, making their divine natures ours, well done, old farmer.

Purpose of Mortality

Lord Byron wrote the line, "Let me but / Be taught the mystery of my being."[200] You are a mystery. We are all mysteries to ourselves. Yet, through Christ, the mystery of who we are and what we will become can be revealed.

We have a divine origin, as children of God, and a divine destiny. President Boyd K. Packer taught, "You are a child of God. He is the father of your spirit. Spiritually you are of noble birth, the offspring of the King of Heaven. Fix that truth in your mind and hold to it. However many generations in your mortal ancestry, no matter what race or people you represent, the pedigree of your spirit can be written on a single line. You are a child of God!"[201]

Because of who we are as the "offspring of the King of Heaven," we are struck from a divine spark and nurtured and reared in divine realms by a greater and holier light. This divine destiny is sometimes disguised to us as we pass through this veil of tears to gain an experiential knowledge of good and evil to become as God. C. S. Lewis reminded us, "It is a serious thing to live in a society of possible gods and goddesses, to remember that the dullest and most uninteresting person you talk to may one day be a creature which, if you saw it now, you would be strongly tempted to worship. . . . You have never talked to a mere mortal."[202]

"All the World's a Stage"

Shakespeare penned the words, "All the world's a stage, / And all the men and women merely players; / They have their exits and their entrances, / And one man in his time plays many parts, / His acts being seven ages."[203]

Shakespeare also identified seven stages of life where we make an entrance, spend some time on that stage, and then exit stage right. Each stage can be seen as a new opportunity for development and experience. His seven stages include infancy ("mewling and puking in the nurse's arms"); schoolchild, apprehensive about leaving his protective home ("with his satchel / And shining morning face, creeping like snail / Unwillingly to school"); lover, who is emotional and musing about his feelings ("sighing like furnace, with a woeful ballad / Made to his mistress' eyebrow"); soldier, where he begins to thinks less of himself and more of others but is somewhat hotheaded and working to make a reputation for himself as a man ("full of strange oaths, and bearded like the pard, / Jealous in honour, sudden, and quick in quarrel"); justice, where he is older and has acquired wisdom, respect, and prosperity ("full of wise saws, and modern instances"); old age, where the bloom begins to wear off the rose and he begins to lose physical and mental ability ("with spectacles on nose and pouch on side, / His youthful hose, well saved, a world too wide / For his shrunk shank"); and finally second childishness, where the man loses his status and becomes a nonentity who is dependent on others ("mere oblivion, / Sans teeth, sans eyes, sans taste, sans everything").[204]

A man or woman plays many parts on this stage created for us by a loving Heavenly Father to develop within us His powers of life. As we pass from stage to stage, we gain new insights and experiences. The French poet Anatole France said, "All changes, even the most longed for, have their melancholy; for what we leave behind us is a part of ourselves; we must die to one life before we can enter another."[205] In life, we live within the range of contradictions of joy and the bittersweetness of experience. We pause in our everyday lives and ask, "Are the joyful moments worth the hard moments?" Shakespeare cynically opined, "Life's but a walking shadow, a poor player / That struts and frets his hour upon the stage / And then is heard no more. It is a tale / Told by an idiot, full of sound and fury, / Signifying nothing."[206]

A Complex System of Genetics and Spirit

Within what Socrates called a "prison house," referring to our physical bodies and minds, we are free to act. Yet we must act within the context of forces working upon us, including predispositions, yearnings, cultures, negative thought patterns, heredity, and so on.

Modern psychology teaches that there are two main forces at work upon us that shape personality: biology and environment. Elder Neal A. Maxwell taught, "Genes and environment by themselves will never provide an adequate explanation for human differences because there is a third factor in the equation of this life: all that occurred before we came here . . . trailing traits from our lengthy and experience in the premortal existence."[207]

In addition to what we bring with us from premortality, there are a host of other factors that influence our lives here on earth. LDS psychologist Allen E. Bergin, PhD, in his book *Eternal Values and Personal Growth* identified seven psychosocial themes that guide our social and emotional facets of our lives. Dr. Bergin developed the following seven themes based on psychological theories and teachings on the spiritual development and capacity of man.[208]

Theme 1: Eternal identity versus the mortal overlay—we have an indestructible personal nature that persists through time and eternity and has infinite potential. This eternal identity is partially obscured by a mortal veil and can progress or regress.

Theme 2: Agency versus impairment—we have the capacity to choose good over evil and exercise our will creatively. Poor choices, abnormal biology, or a pathological or abusive environment can impair this capacity.

Theme 3: Integrity versus deception—acting with sensitivity to the Spirit of Truth makes us more psychologically and spiritually healthy, while acting with deceit, pretense, and betrayal moves us away from such health.

Theme 4: Benevolent power versus unrighteous dominion—when we are in a position of authority or influence, we can serve others through love, persuasion, and sacrifice, or we can control, dominate, and coerce.

Theme 5: Faithful intimacy versus infidelity and self-focus—true love can develop only within a framework of principles that create a lawful structure for expressing affection and creating bonds of loyalty. Ignoring this framework through infidelity and self-centered intimacy create false love, sorrows, and pain.

Theme 6: Marriage, family, and community versus alienation and isolation—faithful love and intimacy are ideally expressed through marriage, family, and commitment to the social community, while extreme individualism results in alienation and isolation.

Theme 7: Progression versus stagnation: eternal values as a framework for growth and adjustment—efforts to become more like God are part of the gospel principle of progression toward exaltation, while inertia and self-satisfaction lead to stagnation or regression. God-given values guide healthy growth, while ethical relativism yields confusion and self-justification.

Bergin commented,

> The more enlightened we become about the shaping forces around us and inside us, the freer we become. The purer our hearts and the more righteous our conduct, the more receptive we are to divine illumination about our circumstances and the alternatives before us with their diverse consequences. . . . By being born again into a newness of life, provided by the Lord's redeeming and healing power, the vision of our possibilities is clarified and our ability to harmonize our lives with eternal light and truth is enhanced.[209]

To Allen Bergin's point, we are not guaranteed absolute freedom in this world. Part of Heavenly Father's plan in this mortal sphere is to encounter problems, stressors, injustices, contradictions, paradoxes, and more.[210] Life is not about survival. It's about experiential learning with the aid of heaven. As we encounter life's challenges, we develop a knowledge of good and evil and learn to prize the good. The Lord instructed Adam, "They taste the bitter, that they may know to prize the good" (Moses 6:55). There are many biological, social, mental, and other forces working upon us. But we have freedom of thought and, in many cases, freedom of action.

Through the exercise of agency, we create something of ourselves. We are independent beings—created in God's image, but still individualistic.

Conclusion: "Gone the Way of All the Earth"

In this life, we are born pure and innocent into a world of promise and discovery. Our consciousness of the world and ourselves unfolds slowly as days and years pass. By the design of our Father in Heaven, we acquire more insights and intellectual abilities as we pass through the days of childhood to adolescence to young adulthood to maturity—and then to where our hard-fought mental and emotional capacities diminish.

W. B. Yeats said, "When you are old and gray and full of sleep, and nodding by the fire, take down this book and slowly read, and dream of the soft look your eyes had once, and of their shadows deep."[211]

So in the end, at least for our mortal selves, "To every thing there is a season, and a time to every purpose under the heaven: a time to be born, and a time to die" (Ecclesiastes 3:1–2).

Chapter 23
The Dark History of Mankind's Ideas and the Light of the Restoration

"Religion is the sigh of the oppressed creature, the heart of a heartless world, and the soul of soulless conditions. It is the opium of the people. The abolition of religion as the illusory happiness of the people is the demand for their real happiness."[212]

Why was the Restoration necessary? Aren't all religions good? Don't they contain some truth?

Some argue that Newton, given the time and technology available to him, was the greatest scientist who ever lived.[213] He postulated the three laws of motion and the law of universal gravitation. He experimented with light and optics. He invented calculus. He is known as the father of the scientific method, a technique for investigating phenomena with empirical and measurable evidence (rejecting Aristotle's appeal to reason and authority to establish fact).

Newton died in 1727, at which time John Conduitt, the executor of Newton's will, published a few of Newton's religious writings, which quickly found their way into obscurity. However, in 1936, the remainder of Newton's works were discovered and published, revealing a deeply religious man. He studied the Bible and the writings of early Christian fathers. In his religious writings, Newton rejected the Trinity, defining "the Father, the Son, and the Holy Spirit; one God in three persons"—distinct beings, yet one "substance, essence or nature."[214]

Against the tradition at the time, he refused to be ordained in the Anglican church. This unpopular decision nearly resulted in his dismal from Cambridge. Much of Newton's writing center on the Apostasy from original Christian doctrines contained in the New Testament. He believed that the original Christian doctrines would be restored. He wrote, "So then the mystery of this restitution of all things is to be found in all the Prophets: which makes me wonder with great admiration that so few Christians of our age can find it there."[215]

Experiment on My Words

To say the least, Newton was a forward thinker for his time. As previously discussed, Newton's scientific method rejected the prevailing notion that matters of science and religion could be decided by an appeal to authority. A common saying of the day *ipse dixit* (Latin for "he himself said it") was the appeal to authority. In its place, Newton encouraged experiments not just in science but also religion.

Just as Newton encouraged experimentation to discover truth, we can also experiment upon the words of Christ. The Book of Mormon prophet Alma encouraged, "Awake and arouse your faculties, even to an experiment upon my words, and exercise a particle of faith" (Alma 32:27).

Using the analogy of a seed that needs exposure to light and the appropriate environment to germinate, sprout, and grow—ever reaching toward the light and absorbing its life-giving qualities—we too need to place a seed of faith in our hearts. Alma instructed, as we feel the spirit within us swell, we know that a cause-and-effect reaction has occurred, and we can say to ourselves, "It must needs be that this is a good seed, or that the word is good, for it beginneth to enlarge my soul; yea, it beginneth to enlighten my understanding, yea, it beginneth to be delicious to me" (Alma 32:28).

Newton wrote, "Let me therefore beg of thee not to trust to the opinion of any man concerning these things, for so it is great odds but thou shalt be deceived. Much less oughtest thou to keep to rely upon the judgment of the multitude, for so thou shalt be deceived. But search the Scriptures thyself and that by frequent reading and constant meditation upon what thou readest, and prayer to God to enlighten thine understanding if thou desirest to find the truth."[216]

Akin to Newton's formula of testing to receive divine truth, on a spring morning in 1820, a young man searching for truth knelt in a grove of trees. "When the light rested upon me I saw two Personages, whose brightness and glory defy all description, standing above me in the air" (Joseph Smith—History 1:17).

Another Dispensation Ushered In

In this fallen world, people corrupt things. Not only do physical objects—if not constantly cared for—tend to decay and break into their constituent parts, but religious ideas and institutions also tend to become perverted as humankind modify original truths and practices commanded from heaven. The gospel of Jesus Christ proclaimed to Adam and Eve was distorted from a sacrifice of a specific animal as a similitude of the sacrifice of the Only Begotten Son to human sacrifice, in some cases. Faith changed into strange superstition. Love for all mankind became corrupted into bigotry, as religions and races claimed superiority over others.

Case in point: The gospel of love was perverted to a gospel of fear. From the New Testament, we read, "Love thy neighbour as thyself" (Mark 12:31), "God is love; and he that dwelleth in love dwelleth in God" (1 John 4:16), and "Beloved, if God so loved us, we ought also to love one another" (1 John 4:11). However, church fathers and theologians by the third and fourth centuries chose to focus on their own misinterpretations of the scriptures. In 2 Thessalonians 1:8, we read, "In flaming fire taking vengeance on them that know not God." For power and to control other people, certain theologians misapplied scriptures about everlasting punishment to the mass of humanity when they do not apply to them.

For example, the Restoration teaches that all God's children, with the minor exception of the sons of perditions, will be resurrected and receive a kingdom of glory: "Ye who are quickened by a portion of the celestial glory shall then receive of the same, even a fulness. And they who are quickened by a portion of the terrestrial glory shall then receive of the same, even a fulness. And also they who are quickened by a portion of the telestial glory shall then receive of the same, even a fulness" (D&C 88:29–31).

Philosopher Alfred North Whitehead remarked, "Another unfortunate consequence of the Reformation was that reformers like Luther and Calvin helped to fixate on large sections of Christendom on the old concept of a 'Divine Despot with a slavish universe, each with the morals of its kind.' "[217] In effect, the early church leaders molded God into the false image more akin to Satan—an unfeeling tyrant who demanded strict obedience. Moses experienced Satan, who cried "with a loud voice, and ranted upon the earth, and commanded, saying: I am the Only Begotten, worship me" (Moses 1:19).

Contrast Satan's maniacal desire to be worshipped with Heavenly Father's loving concern for the people of Enoch's day: "And it came to pass that the God of heaven looked upon the residue of the people, and he wept; and Enoch bore record of it, saying: . . . How is it that thou canst weep, seeing thou art holy, and from all eternity to all eternity? And were it possible that man could number the particles of the earth, yea, millions of earths like this, it would not be a beginning to the number of thy creations; and thy curtains are stretched out still" (Moses 7:28–30). Heavenly Father responded to Enoch's question of how He could weep by stating that we are His children, "the workmanship of [His] own hands" (Moses 7:32).

Not all religious men and leaders perverted the true gospel and concepts on the nature of God. After learning of the decision of the Nicene Council that God was without body, parts, or passions, "Sarapion, a monk of high distinction, prostrated himself on the ground, weeping: 'they have taken my God from me, and I have now none to behold, and whom to worship and address I know not.' "[218]

In the New Testament, we read of the resurrected Christ saying to the Apostles, "Go ye into all the world, and preach the gospel to every creature" (Mark 16:15). However, Christian theologians have taught, even today, that if a person is not fortunate enough to hear the gospel of Christ preached in his or her lifetime, it was God's will and he or she will enter hell upon death and reside there eternally. Both the Calvinists and Arminians taught that those people who escape the eternal flames of the lake of fire and brimstone will rejoice as they watch those who are being endlessly tormented. Thomas Aquinas said, "That the saints may enjoy their beatitude more thoroughly, and give more abundant thanks to God for it, a perfect sight of punishment of the damned is granted them."[219]

A restoration of truth was necessary to counter mankind's false teachings. Just one point of light in the Restoration is that the ordinance of baptism is extended to all of God's children from. The Prophet Joseph Smith, in his funeral sermon for Seymour Brunson, addressed a mother who had lost an unbaptized son and called the doctrine of baptism for the dead "glad tidings of great joy."[220]

Religion Explained Away

The shining heavenly light of the return of the gospel in 1830 was pivotal as religion in the nineteenth century was being dismissed and explained away.

"God is dead. God remains dead. And we have killed him," wrote Friedrich Nietzsche.[221] His point was that Western society no longer relied on religion as a source of meaning or as a moral director. Others joined the chorus that religion is dead and even was a man-made invention of control by religious leaders, which Nietzsche also believed. According to him, the clergy, resentful at their place in the lower social strata, convinced the wealthy and powerful that meekness, humility, and weakness are the true virtues and that they represented the oppressed. This made the clergy morally superior, putting them in a position of power.

Freud said that man actually created a God to worship from the psychological defense mechanism of infantile regression. Desiring a powerful father figure to care for us and help us control violent impulses, we created God—not the other way around. Freud additionally believed that religious impulses arose from a shadowy memory of our experiences as small children, before we could speak and when our individual self was undefined. Spiritual feelings of closeness to God, to Freud, were memories resurfacing from our first years of life, when we felt secure and at one with our fathers and mothers.

Speaking of conscience, Freud—with his belief in naturalism and the theories of evolution of his day—promulgated the view that people are naturally aggressive, like earlier, primal ancestors. The phenomenon called conscience was simply the product of the mind. Over time, people learned to control impulses of aggression and violence toward one another so they could live in harmony in a modern society.

Other ideas forthcoming in the nineteenth century, leading into the twentieth century, included determinism, relativism, and nihilism.

Determinism is the philosophy that events have causes and that even human choices are caused. Determinism is often contrasted with free will. This philosophy states that events, including the actions and choices of humans, are determined by preceding events, so true freedom of choice is impossible.

However, the Restoration teaches that men and women are free to think and act, "according to the moral agency which I have given unto him, that every man may be accountable for his own sins in the day of judgment" (D&C 101:78). The Lord has spoken of giving Adam and Eve their agency: "I gave unto them their knowledge, in the day I created them; and in the Garden of Eden, gave I unto man his agency" (Moses 7:32). It is Satan's desire "to destroy the agency of man" (Moses 4:3).

From the discoveries of Newton up to the early twentieth century, scientists believed that the universe was deterministic. Once all the scientific laws were discovered, everything in the universe, from human behavior to the formation of stars, could be determined, and even the future could be predicted. Therefore, under determinism, no agency or free will could exist.

But leading into the twentieth century, the uncertainty principle was discovered. This principle states there are limits on how accurately things can be measured. The classic example is measuring the position and speed of an individual electron. Scientists can make a prediction on how the electrons as a group will act under certain conditions, but they cannot predict what individual electrons will do, causing uncertainty.

David V. Dearden, professor of biochemistry at Brigham Young University, said,

> I find it fascinating that the biochemistry of thought and decision making, of signal transmission in neurons, occurs at the level of electrons and atoms, where quantum uncertainty operates and behavior is not deterministic. At this level we can't always predict exactly what will happen. Therefore this basic idea of quantum mechanics suggests that our thoughts and decisions are not deterministic.
>
> At the same time, uncertainty only becomes important for very small particles like electrons and atoms. For larger things, we can make accurate predictions. This is important too—otherwise, all would be chaos. Instead, after we make choices, consequences inevitably follow.

> Therefore, we live in a universe that is predictable enough that our actions have consequences but not so predictable that it is deterministic.
>
> It is as if the Lord designed the very fabric of the universe in such a way as to guarantee us the opportunity of agency while still demanding consequences to the way we use our agency. Thus not only do we live in a universe that is "just right" to allow human existence, it is also "just right" to give us the sacred gift of agency.[222]

Another form of determinism is naturalism, the philosophy that people are natural objects governed by biological and chemical processes that explain human behavior, leaving little room for agency. Naturalism views people as living organisms determined by natural laws. Human behavior is the result of physiological causes within environmental conditions.

Determinism, the view that all is predetermined and that mankind has little to no agency, taken to its logical end, contradicts the promises of the opened-ended, infinite, and eternal gospel. "For, behold, the mystery of godliness, how great is it! For, behold, I am endless" (D&C 19:10).

The modern ideas of the twentieth century and absolute determinism eventually were turned upside down by postmodern thinkers. In a swing the other direction, postmodernism holds that human beings create their own lives through the meaning they attach to events as they process reality. We really are meaning-making machines, assigning emotions and feelings to events and people, reshuffling meanings as we try to make sense of life. But if we manufacture a world inside our minds, then there is no certainty, objective reality, or absolute truth.

All this creation of meaning led to the philosophy of existentialism and the individual construction of reality. Existentialism is the belief that true psychological awareness begins within the person and a sense of disorientation about the world. People in search of the true meaning of life reach the point where they see the world for what it is: meaningless or absurd. Søren Kierkegaard, considered to be the first existentialist philosopher, believed that individuals, not their culture, society, or religion, gave meaning to their lives. Then by living "authentically" to this meaning they created for themselves (living sincerely and passionately), they would find happiness.[223] This belief has heavily influenced philosophy and religion of today.

However, is the individual the best judge of reality? Who's to say my self-constructed moral and ethical system is better than yours? Therefore, existentialism eliminates any standard of truth. But there is a standard. Truth is not relative. "All truth is independent in that sphere in which God has placed it" (D&C 93:30).

A form of existentialism is nihilism, the denial of real existence or possibility of objective truth. Nihilism means nothingness or nonexistence.[224] This philosophical approach holds that not only is life meaningless, but religion, cultural mores, and political systems are utterly devoid of meaning. In a world where truth exists but is not forced upon us, this is like being "tossed to and fro, and carried about with every wind of doctrine, by the sleight of men, and cunning craftiness, whereby they lie in wait to deceive; but speaking the truth in love, may grow up into him in all things, which is the head, even Christ" (Ephesians 4:14–15). The Savior said, "I am the way, the truth, and the life: no man cometh unto the Father, but by me" (John 14:6).

Convincing mankind that there is nothing to existence or reality is Satan's clarion call. The idea that there is no meaning in our mortal experience, or life after death, creates despair and hopelessness. To quiet the distressing voices of our souls as we call out for meaning in the face of the belief that life is devoid of meaning, sin seems the great escape—albeit temporary escape, with consequences ready to clutch us in their toothy jaws. Where nihilism offers darkness in its deepest black, the restored gospel offers the souls of mankind the whitest, brightest light.

There are no religious creeds in the Church's theology. The Prophet Joseph Smith undoubtedly taught Brigham Young, who said that " 'Mormonism' includes all truth. There is no truth but what belongs to the gospel."[225] After seeing the Father and the Son and receiving revelation upon revelation from Them, Joseph Smith acknowledged the Godhead as the source of all divine truth, not mankind's interpretation of scriptures.

The history of the Restoration is based on divine appearances—actual events and experiences with heaven, including the First Vision and visitations of resurrected and translated beings like Moroni; John the Baptist; Peter, James, and John; Moses; Elijah; Elias; and others. And not to mention Joseph Smith receiving metal plates containing over a thousand years an ancient writings, covering the religious and social history of two civilizations and containing plain and precious truths previously lost to the world.

From all of this, the Prophet Joseph said, "The Standard of Truth has been erected; no unhallowed hand can stop the work from progressing; persecutions may rage, mobs may combine, armies may assemble, calumny may defame, but the truth of God will go forth boldly, nobly, and independent, till it has penetrated every continent, visited every clime, swept every country, and sounded in every ear, till the purposes of God shall be accomplished and the Great Jehovah shall say the work is done."[226]

Just like Enoch, Noah, Abraham, and Moses, the world needed yet another restoration. Speaking of the final restoration of truth before the Savior's Second Coming, President Spencer W. Kimball taught, "After centuries of spiritual darkness . . . we solemnly announce to all the world that the spiritual famine is ended, the spiritual drought is spent, the word of the Lord in its purity and totalness is available to all men. One needs not wander from sea to sea nor from the north to the east, seeking the true gospel as Amos predicted, for the everlasting truth is available."[227]

Chapter 24
Seeing the World through Two Different Lenses

"Religion is a system of wishful illusions together with a disavowal of reality, such as we find nowhere else but in a state of blissful hallucinatory confusion. Religion's eleventh commandment is 'Thou shalt not question.' "[228]

"Looking for God—or Heaven—by exploring space is like reading or seeing all Shakespeare's plays in the hope that you will find Shakespeare as one of the characters or Stratford as one of the places. Shakespeare is in one sense present at every moment in every play."[229]

Are mankind's beliefs and behaviors rooted not in the existence of a divine Creator but in the psychology of the mind? Or is there a spiritual and supernatural dimension to life that, once I find the door, offers heavenly rays of enlightenment?

As we start the conclusion of this book, let's go back to C. S. Lewis and where we began.

I hope I've taken you on a journey similar to that of C. S. Lewis, the great Christian writer, as he reexamined his life as an atheist and found Christ.

From the eternal truths and principles revealed through the Restoration of the gospel presented in this book, I hope you received similar spiritual insights that led Lewis to a spiritual transformation and belief in Christ as the source of truth, purpose, and meaning in life.

In these pages, I've tried to help you take another look at the meaningful truths of the restored gospel of Jesus Christ and how they answer many of the great questions of life. It is my greatest desire that the eternal truths in this book help to rekindle the Light of Christ and give you flashes of insight to your divine potential and sense of your destiny as a daughter or son of God.

There is power in the message of the restored gospel. The heavens are abundantly open again in preparation for the Second Coming! Speaking of American philosopher Ralph Waldo Emerson, Elder Jeffery R. Holland said,

> The incomparable Ralph Waldo Emerson rocked the very foundations of New England ecclesiastical orthodoxy when he said to the Divinity School at Harvard: "It is my duty to say to you that the need was never greater [for] new revelation than now." "The doctrine of inspiration is lost. . . . Miracles, prophecy, . . . the holy life, exist as ancient history [only]. . . . Men have come to speak of . . . revelation as somewhat long ago given and done, as if God were dead. . . . It is the office of a true teacher," he warned, "to show us that God is, not was; that He speaketh, not spake." In essence, Mr. Emerson was saying, "If you persist in handing out stones when people ask for bread, they will eventually stop coming to the bakery."
>
> Consider these stunning indictments from the towering figures of American history . . . and it highlights in bold relief the powerful message of The Church of Jesus Christ of Latter-day Saints. . . . Prophets? Seers? Revelators? The events of 1820 and 1830, and the events of nearly two centuries that have followed, declare that revelations and those who receive them are not "long ago given and done."
>
> In the very year Mr. Emerson gave his Divinity School address implicitly pleading for such, Elder John Taylor, a young English immigrant to this country, was called to be an Apostle of the Lord Jesus Christ, a prophet, a seer, a revelator. In that calling Elder Taylor once said in sympathy with honest seekers of truth: "Whoever heard of true religion without communication with God? To me the thing is the most absurd that the human mind could conceive of. I do not wonder," said Brother Taylor, "[that] when the people generally reject the principle of present revelation, skepticism and infidelity prevail to such an alarming extent. I do not wonder," he continued, "that so many

men treat religion with contempt, and regard it as something not worth the attention of intelligent beings, for without revelation religion is a mockery and a farce. . . . *The principle of present revelation . . . is the very foundation of our religion.*"[230]

The Question of God

Professor and psychiatrist Dr. Armand Nicholi teaches one of the most popular courses at Harvard University. From the course emerged the PBS documentary *The Question of God: Sigmund Freud & C. S. Lewis*.

Nicholi said, "Freud and Lewis are two brilliant men with two different ideas of human existence. Lewis and Freud represent conflicting sides of ourselves. Whatever part we choose will determine our purpose, identity, and our whole philosophy of life."[231] He allows both sides to be represented. "Religion is the universal obsessional neurosis of humanity," said Freud, representing the secular humanist view of life. "It has been my life's work to show man that his beliefs and behaviors are rooted not in divine truth but in his own childhood fears and desires." Lewis, representing the Christian theistic view, said, "I believe in God as I believe the sun has risen. Not because I can see it, but by way of it I can see everything else."

In Nicholi's course, he contrasts the views of the scientific-minded Freud with the philosophical- and religious-minded Lewis, juxtaposing science and religion into two neatly divided camps.

Sigmund Freud

As a boy, Freud lived in a religious home, steeped in the beliefs of a community of Eastern European Jews, who lived among a majority of Catholics. Family life, school, and religion were interwoven in this place at this point in history. As a small boy, he learned to read from the Bible in Hebrew. At this time, his father was in the wool business and prospered. The family hired a nursemaid for Sigmund, who took him to churches and told him a "great deal about God Almighty and hell. She took [him] to church and when [he] got home [he] would preach to family about what God Almighty does."

When he was a young man, the wool industry collapsed and the Freud family fell on tough economic times. They moved from Frieberg to Vienna to live in a ghetto. His father, knowing Sigmund was gifted intellectually, hired a tutor, who gave Freud a love of the humanities and Jewish history. Next, he went on to secondary school and entered the world of German secularism. Scientific teaching captivated Freud's young imagination. In the second half of the nineteenth century, more and more natural phenomena were being explained scientifically, not supernaturally. Religious institutions felt threatened, marking this time a war between science and religion.

Freud said of this time of his life, "I felt an overpowering need to understand something of the riddles of the world in which we live and perhaps even to contribute something to their solution. . . . I came to know all the fields of science."

C. S. Lewis

As mentioned at the beginning of this book, C. S. Lewis experienced a spiritual transformation from a reasoned atheist to a devout Christian intellectual, whose writings have filled the world. At the preparatory school Cherbourg House, he rejected his Christian beliefs and became an atheist. Lewis's atheism became further entrenched as he served on the front lines in the Somme Valley in France, dealing firsthand with the fear of dying and witnessing death taking young and promising lives.

After the war, Lewis returned to Oxford University as a student and later as faculty, serving in the English department along with J. R. R. Tolkien. Lewis became good friends with his respected colleague, who was a devout Catholic. They took walks into the woods and discussed religion and mythology. Lewis remarked that as he talked with Tolkien, he felt his atheistic constructs beginning to give way. He came to slowly know Christ in intimate ways. He said of his conversion, "It came up from behind and took over my heart." He could sense that something was happening to him and he was caught up in the flow of the experience.

Lewis's and Freud's Different Views on Life

In his Harvard course, Nicholi presents,

> Both Lewis and Freud thought deep and wide about many important issues: the meaning and purpose of life, the nature of morality, true happiness, human sexuality, suffering and pain, and the existence of God. On nearly all of these issues the two thinkers came to quite different

> conclusions. . . . Both men were gifted with formidable intellects and wrote widely. Both suffered significant losses in their early years. Both had conflicts with their fathers. Both had a religious upbringing which they later repudiated. Lewis later abandoned his atheism and converted to Christianity, while Freud remained an atheist.[232]

Freud's views on existence were materialistic and naturalistic. Lewis's were spiritual and supernatural. Freud believed the world and its contents could be explained exclusively in terms of physical causes. Lewis argued the world and its contents could be augmented by the spiritual.

Freud attacked religion as ignorant and childish on psychological grounds. "The notions of God and the spiritual are simply wish-fulfillments and human projections of inner needs. As such they are illusions and false beliefs. When people become more educated they will abandon such juvenile concepts as the divine and the supernatural."[233]

Lewis viewed religion and discipleship as not an easy or delightful life decision. "Many of the demands of the Christian worldview are not something a person would wish for. The Gospels inform us that followers of Jesus must abandon their own desires and die to self," said Lewis, contradicting Freud. "The Christian faith never promises the absence of pain and suffering: quite the opposite. We are told to expect persecution and admonished to take up our cross and follow Jesus."

Could Freud's wish fulfillment be a desire for a connection with the divine, a buried memory of the love of Father in Heaven that existed from premortality? Is the human desire to reach upward for the transcendent the same as projecting psychological images of childhood fathers and longing to be with the ideal father again? As Lewis said, "If I find in myself a desire which no experience in this world can satisfy, the most probable explanation is that I was made for another world."[234]

Of course, Freud is most widely known for his views on sex. And as in other areas, his thinking differs markedly from Lewis. The views of Freud on human sexuality are well known. In his defense, Freud seemed more interested in the freedom to speak about sex than to necessarily act on sex. However, Lewis challenged Freud's idea that sexual repression can lead to neuroses. Lewis said repression is not the same as suppression. Suppression is the conscious control of one's impulses—a necessary component of civilization. It is not the control of sexuality that is unhealthy, but rather the lack of control.

Not surprisingly, Freud felt that real happiness was primarily tied up in the satisfaction of sexual needs. Lewis thought otherwise. Lewis felt that happiness will always be elusive if directly sought after. It can be obtained as a byproduct if we live our lives in accordance with our design. And we are designed to have a relationship with our Creator. Indeed, argued Lewis, all our attempts to obtain happiness will fail until we realize the primary purpose of our lives: to be in relationship with God, who made us.

Conclusion: Who's Right?

Which view best explains the world we find ourselves in, and which one gives us a proper grounding for hope, meaning, and true satisfaction?

How can we definitely know that God exists and why He created us with all these yearnings to understand ourselves and fulfill our destinies? In this great debate, the side we choose influences so much of how we see our identities and purpose in life. Is it easier not to believe, to not need to exercise faith and solve the God riddle and ponder deep things at the edge of consciousness?

Chapter 25
The Mystery of Life and Your Being

"To become what we are capable of becoming is the only end in life."[235]

As C. S. Lewis referred to, how does a person really know that God exists? Is it easier not to believe, to not ponder deep things about the mystery of my being?

Let's wrap this up where we began: in a small region in Armenia, an earthquake devastated a city. A father ran quickly to his son's school. Breathlessly reaching the structure, now a pile of rubble, he began frantically yet carefully to remove the broken pieces of the building. There were no signs of life.

When others told him to stop because it was hopeless, he said he had made a promise to his son that no matter what, he would always be there. He continued to remove the rubble from where he estimated his son's classroom had been. Other parents cried and wailed but did not help him.

He removed rubble for thirty-eight hours when he heard voices. "Armand!" he screamed. He heard his son reply, "Dad! It's me . . . Armand!" His son continued, "I told the other kids not to worry. I told them that if you were alive, you'd save me, and when you saved me, they'd be saved. You promised you would always be there for me. You did it, Dad!" The father helped his son and thirteen other boys and girls from the debris.[236]

As I stated earlier in this book, Heavenly Father, through Christ, reached patiently and lovingly out to C. S. Lewis, just as the Armenia father searched for his son through the rubble and would not stop until he had reached his son. The rubble in Lewis's life included his mother dying at a young age, experiencing the horrors of World War I, and other events.

Reflecting on his conversion from atheism to Christianity, Lewis commented that he could "feeling the unrelenting approach of someone he did not desire to meet."[237]

Heavenly Father has done the same for me, reaching through the rubble of my life that I create by poor decisions and not living up to my divine potential. But most important, he found me and set me on a path leading closer to Him and His Son.

Heavenly Father is reaching out to you as well! He really is. In His own way, respecting the dimensions of your faith and agency, Heavenly Father's "hand is stretched out still" (Isaiah 10:4).

But how can you know this? Why does it seem so difficult? What are you to do?

You begin by searching through the rubble of your life, removing the broken pieces of cement and twisted steel of preconceived doubts and worldly ideas and philosophies, and open yourself to experience God.

You do this by honest, open, sincere truth-seeking, as C. S. Lewis did and countless other people have done, and by having a willingness to accept the truth, whatever that may be.

In your quiet moments, the yearnings to know of yourself and the mystery of your being are purposeful. Heavenly Father put them there. Additionally, people unwittingly experience varying degrees of celestial homesickness—the desire to be made whole as they once were in His celestial presence.

Sister Eliza R. Snow understood this when she penned the lines of the following hymn, "For a wise and glorious purpose / Thou hast placed me here on earth / And withheld the recollection / Of my former friends and birth; / Yet ofttimes a secret something / Whispered, 'You're a stranger here,' / And I felt that I had wandered / From a more exalted sphere."[238]

Embrace Truth to Change Our Natures

The Prophet Joseph Smith once posed the question, "Who has duly considered the condescension of the Father of our spirits, in providing a sacrifice for His creatures, a plan of redemption, a power of atonement . . . [and] the bringing of men back into the presence of the King of heaven"?[239]

One of the purposes of life is to embrace truth. In our fallen condition, we may, through Christ, receive the divine endowments of truth, intelligence, and light that comprise celestial glory and power. "Ye who are quickened by a portion of the celestial glory shall then receive of the same, even a fulness" (D&C 88:29). "And thus we saw the glory of the celestial, which excels in all things—where God, even the Father, reigns upon his throne forever and ever" (D&C 76:92).

By relying on Christ, we are given divine power to overcome the world and bring attributes of eternal life into our beings. To do so, we must embrace and live truth. "And if a person gains more knowledge and intelligence in this life through his diligence and obedience than another, he will have so much the advantage in the world to come" (D&C 130:19).

This is how we become "independent above all other creatures beneath the celestial world" (D&C 78:14). We are taught, "For if you will that I give unto you a place in the celestial world, you must prepare yourselves by doing the things which I have commanded you and required of you" (D&C 78:7).

Articulating the reason and need for all of us to come unto Christ, Joseph Smith said, "As the Son partakes of the fulness of the Father through the Spirit, so the saints are, by the same Spirit, to be partakers of the same fulness, to enjoy the same glory."[240] The entire purpose of the gospel is to bring men back into the presence of the Father in glorified resurrected states—celestial, terrestial, or telestial in nature.

Becoming Sons and Daughters of Christ

All men and women in mortality will die, and all will be resurrected. In the resurrection, we will have the opportunity to receive everlasting life: "If they be good, to the resurrection of everlasting life; and if they be evil, to the resurrection of damnation" (3 Nephi 26:5).

Resurrection to everlasting life allows us to receive an endowment of the glory and power of God. This is how we become like God, through the bestowal of His life-developing, life-regenerating, life-expanding powers, and this happens through celestial resurrection. All other resurrections are resurrections of damnation because eternal progression is halted, just as a dam holds back massive amounts of water and energy.

Another way of referring to the everlasting life of celestial resurrection is becoming the sons and daughters of Christ. The Savior said, "But to as many as received me, gave I power to become my sons; and even so will I give unto as many as will receive me, power to become my sons" (D&C 39:4). For those willing to pay the price of discipleship, coming unto Christ in obedience and love, He provides His Spirit to help us overcome the corruptness and carnality of our fallen natures.

Just as the Savior "received not of the fulness at first, but continued from grace to grace, until he received a fulness" (D&C 93:13), through Him we are continuing from grace to grace, and He will remain with us through our trials and tribulations, our spiritual growth spurts and recessions, until we receive of the fulness of His characteristics, attributes, powers, and more endlessly. Remember, Christ "received all power, both in heaven and on earth, and the glory of the Father was with him, for he dwelt in him" (D&C 93:17).

Hence all the references to "rebirth" and being "born again" in the scriptures. By being born again, we are given divine spiritual endowments that enable us to receive new life spiritually. And these spiritual endowments come as we live the gospel and keep covenants, transforming us and taking away our fallen natures. We become spiritual beings as well as physical beings. The Apostle John said, "As many as received him, to them gave he power to become the sons of God, even to them that believe on his name: which were born, not of blood, nor of the will of the flesh, nor of the will of man, but of God" (John 1:12–13).

Conclusion

What great promises we find in the scriptures. If you have received the Holy Ghost, the "record of heaven" (Moses 6:61)—a knowledge of all things past, present, and future—lies dormant within you. Learn to access it for your future benefit and happiness.

Chapter 26
In Conclusion

"'Look out!' we cry, 'it's *alive*.' And therefore this is the very point at which so many draw back—I would have done so myself if I could—and proceed no further with Christianity. An 'impersonal God'—well and good. A subjective God of beauty, truth and goodness, inside our own heads—better still. A formless life-force surging through us, a vast power which we can tap—best of all. But God Himself, alive, pulling at the other end of the cord, perhaps approaching at an infinite speed, the hunter, king, husband—that is quite another matter."[241]

What is the purpose of life? Is God really searching for me, waiting for me to experience Him?

Scottish legend claims that William Wallace, who led the Scots to independence from the British, stated, "Every man dies. Not every man really lives." American novelist Jack London penned the following words:

> I would rather be ashes than dust!
>
> I would rather that my spark should burn out in a brilliant blaze than it should be stifled by dry-rot.
>
> I would rather be a superb meteor, every atom of me in magnificent glow, than a sleepy and permanent planet.

> The function of man is to live, not to exist.
> I shall not waste my days trying to prolong them.
> I shall use my time.[242]

Through Christ and His Resurrection, we will be more than ashes and dust. We will be light-filled, truth-filled, glory-filled sons and daughters of God—with a knowledge of good and evil gained experientially—prepared to dwell eternally with God, where we will experience more joy than we can now comprehend.

Life Is a Gift to Be Lived!

Life is a gift of eternal significance. Life is to be lived joyfully and authentically, as intended by our Father in Heaven. Yes, even in our moments of discouragement. Why? Because of the Savior and His everlasting gifts to us. The Doctrine and Covenants state,

> Let the mountains shout for joy, and all ye valleys cry aloud; and all ye seas and dry lands tell the wonders of your Eternal King! And ye rivers, and brooks, and rills, flow down with gladness. Let the woods and all the trees of the field praise the Lord; and ye solid rocks weep for joy! And let the sun, moon, and the morning stars sing together, and let all the sons of God shout for joy! And let the eternal creations declare his name forever and ever! And again I say, how glorious is the voice we hear from heaven, proclaiming in our ears, glory, and salvation, and honor, and immortality, and eternal life; kingdoms, principalities, and powers! (D&C 128:33)

Just as God was mindful of C. S. Lewis and provided the spiritual direction to bring him to conversion (all the while respecting Lewis's agency), Heavenly Father is mindful of you.

Here's a case in point. My friend Steve Frye was called to serve in the Bakersfield, California Mission. While his friends were being called to serve in foreign countries, Steve would serve only three hundred miles from his hometown. In his good nature, he said that the best thing about his call was that when he received cookies from home, they were still warm.

Steve passed away at forty-two from stomach cancer. A few weeks before he died, he gave his second farewell talk in the ward where he served as bishop. "I lived pretty much a fairy tale life. I was born into one of the finest families who have ever walked the earth. About seven to eight months ago, I made a quick trip to the hospital because I had a small stomachache. From that stomachache, I was diagnosed with a cancer that they said was quite treatable. I'm a slow learner. If I had been a little smarter, I would have realized that the final chapters in my life were being written."

In his farewell to mortality talk, Steve related an experience about a family living in Russia. The Spirit fell on the family and told them to sell all that they had and buy tickets to anywhere in the West. They ended up in Panama, and from Panama they walked to California. In California, the teenage son Bill became Americanized and married a beautiful American girl.

After three years of marriage, two sister missionaries knocked on their door. The wife listened and was baptized, but Bill declined to be baptized.

One night, the wife had a dream. In that dream, she saw the name on a missionary tag, and a voice told her that when that missionary came to her home, her husband would be baptized. Every Tuesday evening, she had the missionaries to her home dinner for the next seventeen years. Steve was transferred into that area. The wife tapped Steve on the shoulder and he read his nametag: Elder Frye. She burst into tears and ran away. Steve asked his companion if that was how she greeted all the missionaries.

That Tuesday, Steve and his companion had dinner with the family. After dinner, the wife took Steve off into a corner of the kitchen and said that she'd had a dream and learned that when Elder Frye came to her home, her husband would join the Church.

The following Tuesday, Steve came prepared to give the first discussion, asking Bill's permission. He said, "Why not, all the other missionaries who have come here have taught me." They went through about the first half of the discussion when Steve closed the binder and said that was enough for the night. "Go on, Elder Frye, you haven't finished the lesson yet," said Bill. "Yes, we've finished the lesson for tonight." That was Steve's way.

The wife took Steve aside and said, "Elder Frye. you did it all wrong. You didn't finish the concepts. You didn't commit him to pray. You didn't do any of the things you were supposed to do." Steve said to the wife, "Do you believe the dream?" She said she did with all her heart.

Steve finished the fourth lesson. The Spirit was there, but Bill was not committing. Steve said, "Bill what is it that you are looking for?" The man said, "My life is perfect. I have a beautiful wife, three beautiful children, and a successful business. I have my health and strength. There is nothing that could possibly make my life any fuller." Steve said, "What is going to happen when you have an emergency in your life and you need to call down the powers of heaven and the priesthood to bless your family?" He said, "I'll call you or one of the other missionaries." Steve said, "That may not always be an option." He said, "Well, what are you trying to tell me?"

Steve said, "I'm trying to tell you that the Lord is seeing a need to humble you, and if you do not humble yourself, He will humble you for yourself." He asked, "What does that mean?" Steve said, "He may humble you through a child, your spouse, or through you yourself." He asked, "What does that mean?" Steve said, "It means you are supposed to join the Church and be baptized." Bill said, "I don't think I'm ready to do that." Steve said, "Okay." Bill said, "We'll see you next Tuesday night." Steve said, "No, were not coming anymore." That was Steve's way.

Two weeks later, Bill called Steve. "Elder Frye, I had to go to the doctor today. I've been diagnosed with a brain tumor and it's all your fault, so come over here." So Steve and his companion went over to Bill's house. He sat Steve down and said, "Elder Frye. This is all your fault, so I want you to give me a blessing." Steve said, "This is not my fault. It's your fault and the only one who can fix it is you. If you have sufficient faith, we'll give you a blessing."

Steve and his companion gave Bill a blessing. Bill then went into surgery three days later. The doctors found the tumor, and it was a spider tumor, weaving in and out of his brain. They took the end of the tumor and, with a great amount of effort, were able to completely pull the tumor from his skull. The doctors told him when he woke up that it was a miracle.

After the surgery, Steve and his companion came to the hospital. Bill said, "Elder Frye, the doctors say that my wounds and such will be healed enough so that I can be baptized in two weeks. How does that fit with your schedule?"

Here's what I find remarkable about this experience. The Lord knew that my friend Steve would influence Bill in profound ways. It wasn't that Elder Frye was better than any of the other past missionaries who transferred in and out Bill's life. The Lord knew that Steve could reach Bill in a certain way. The Lord led Bill's family from Russia to Panama to the United States. He was doing all of this at the same time that Steve was just a kid growing up in Northern California only a few hundred miles away from Bakersfield, California, being given spiritual experiences to prepare him to teach Bill.

Invitation to Come Back

Perhaps you were baptized and received the priesthood or were faithful in the Young Women's program. You may even have made temple covenants but have strayed from those promises. Despite your current situation, "his [the Lord's] hand is stretched out still" (Isaiah 10:4).

We are all prodigal sons and daughters of our Father in Heaven. No matter who we are, all of us have pridefully wandered away from our true spiritual selves and found out, sooner or later, that we need to return home to the Father who gave us life.

In the Savior's parable, when the hungry and downtrodden prodigal son, with his malnourished, husk-filled stomach, comes into sight of his father's home, his father feels a wave of compassion come over him. The father's next reaction is to not stand on the porch, arms folded across chest, tapping his foot impatiently, rehearsing the "I told you so" scolding he is about to give his son. Like a lightening-fast reflex, the father bounds off the porch and runs. There is a sense of urgency and gladness. "But when he was yet a great way off, his father saw him, and had compassion, and ran, and fell on his neck, and kissed him" (Luke 15:20).

Some people are born believers. Others have a stumbling blocks in their way to simple belief. One person is not better than another. But whoever we are, it is incumbent upon us to come unto Christ. In many cases, we all need to suspend our disbeliefs. As the Book of Mormon teaches, "Wherefore, whoso believeth in God might with surety hope for a better world, yea, even a place at the right hand of God, which hope cometh of faith, maketh an anchor to the souls of men, which would make them sure and steadfast, always abounding in good works, being led to glorify God" (Ether 12:4).

Too many people believe that in life we do our best, and then Christ makes up the difference. Wrong! He makes all the difference *as* we do our best. We need His power to change.

No matter who you are, where you have been, or what you have done, His words to you will not change: "Return unto me, and repent of your sins, and be converted, that I may heal you" (3 Nephi 9:13).

Endnotes

1. Name has been changed.

2. Thomas S. Monson, "Obedience Brings Blessings," *Ensign*, May 2013.

3. William Wordsworth, as quoted in Arthur Quiller-Couch, *The Oxford Book of English Verse* (Oxford: Clarendon, 1919).

4. Boyd J. Petersen, *Hugh Nibley: A Consecrated Life* (Sandy, Utah: Greg Kofford Books, 2002), 56.

5. C. S. Lewis, "Is Theology Poetry," *The Weight of Glory* (New York: HarperOne, 2001), 140.

6. James E. Faust, "'Them That Honour Me I Will Honour,'" *Ensign*, May 2001.

7. Gregory S. Cootsona, *C. S. Lewis and the Crisis of a Christian* (Louisville: Westminster John Knox Press, 2014), 5.

8. C. S. Lewis, *Mere Christianity* (Oxford: Geoffrey Bles, 1952), 8.

9. C. S. Lewis, *Surprised by Joy* (Oxford: Geoffrey Bles, 1955), 215.

10. C. S. Lewis, *Surprised by Joy*, 215.

11. C. S. Lewis, *Surprised by Joy*, 228–29.

12. C. S. Lewis, *The Voyage of the Dawn Treader* (Oxford: Geoffrey Bles, 1952).

13. C. S. Lewis, *The Great Divorce* (Oxford: Geoffrey Bles, 1945).

14. Boyd K. Packer, "A Tribute to the Rank and File of the Church," *Ensign*, May 1980.

15. *Joy* is mentioned 120 times in the Book of Mormon.

16. C. S. Lewis, *Letters to Malcolm: Chiefly on Prayer* (Oxford: Geoffrey Bles, 1964), 90–91.

17. Joseph F. Smith, *Teachings of the Prophet Joseph Smith* (Salt Lake City: Deseret Book, 1977), 255.

18. C. S. Lewis, "Bluspels and Flalansferes: A Semantic Nightmare," *Rehabilitations, and Other Essays* (Oxford: Geoffrey Bles, 1939).

19. C. S. Lewis, *Surprised by Joy*, 180.

20. C. S. Lewis, *Miracles* (New York: HarperOne, 1947), 93–94.

21. C. S. Lewis, *Mere Christianity,* 93–94.

22. Søren Kierkegaard, *Four Upbuilding Discourses, 1844* (Princeton: Princeton University Press, 1844).

23. The *Epic of Gilgamesh* is an epic poem from ancient Mesopotamia. Dating from the Third Dynasty of Ur (circa 2100 BC), it is often regarded as the first great work of literature.

24. *Epic of Gilgamesh*, trans. Danny P. Jackson (Wauconda, Illinois: Bolchazy-Carducci Publishers, 1997), 71.

25. Ibid., 86.

26. Lord Byron, "Cain, a Mystery," *The Major Works*, ed. Jerome J. McGann (Oxford: Oxford University Press, 1986), 140.

27. John Keats, "Letter to George and Georgiana Keats," March 19, 1819, see https://archive.org/stream/lettersofjohnkea00keatiala/lettersofjohnkea00keatiala_djvu.txt.

28. Thomas S. Monson, "Obedience Brings Blessings."

29. Ralph W. Sockman, *Ohio Wesleyan*, 1911.

30. Sarah Gambles, "President Monson tells students to let lights burn brightly," *Deseret News*, November 1, 2011.

31. Clayton M. Christensen, "Decisions for Which I've Been Grateful," BYU–I devotional, June 8, 2004.

32. Terryl Givens, "Letter to a Doubter," http://terrylgivens.com/wp-content/uploads/2010/03/Letter-to-a-Doubter.pdf.

33. Ibid.

34. Ten volumes of the *Anagnoseis* ("Calling to Mind") purport to be Clement's autobiographical account of how he learned the faith from Saint Peter and in turn delivered it to the Church. (Source: *The Ante-Nicene Christian Library*, Vol. 3, 135–471, http://www.biblical.ie/Apocrypha/ClemRecog_1-5.asp#_Toc202084229.)

35. Ibid.

36. *The Collected Works of Hugh Nibley*, Vol. 3 (Provo: FARMS), 11–12.

37. Journal account of Elder Scott Anderson. See http://holyfetch.com/conversions/Gertrude_Specht.html.

38. *Church News*, November 1973, see https://www.lds.org/ensign/1973/11/news-of-the-church?lang=eng. In the year 2000, Professor Daniel Peterson, the director of FARMS (Foundation for Ancient Research and Mormon Studies at BYU) asked Marc A. Schindler (who once was Gertrude Specht's home teacher) to verify the story. Though Brother Schindler was not there when Sister Specht was converted and could not authenticate the story, he said that the journal entry from Elder Anderson is close to the story he remembered Sister Specht telling him about her

conversion. Some facts may have been embellished, but he felt the majority of the story was accurate. Additionally, Jonathan Green a writer for the *Times & Seasons* blog also researched the validity of the Sister Specht story and confirmed her academic achievements and activity in the Church (see http://timesandseasons.org/index.php/2008/05/gertrud-specht/). However, no research can ascertain the validity of all the facts of Elder Scott Anderson's journal account.

39. *Teachings of the Prophet Joseph Smith* (Salt Lake City: Deseret Book, 1977), 353.

40. Joseph Smith, "The King Follett Discourse," *Ensign*, May 1971.

41. *Teachings of the Prophet Joseph Smith*, 343, 354.

42. Ibid., 354.

43. *Journal of Discourses*, Vol. 8 (London: Latter-day Saints' Book Depot, 1854–86), 30.

44. Heinz R. Pagels, *The Cosmic Code: Quantum Physics as the Language of Nature* (Mineola, New York: Dover Publications, 1982), 295.

45. ABC News national broadcast, October 24, 2012, see http://abcnews.go.com/Health/neuroscientist-sees-proof-heaven-week-long-coma/story?id=17555207.

46. "My Heavenly Father Loves Me," *Hymns*, no. 228.

47. Oath against modernism formulated by Pius X, a pope of the Catholic church.

48. Douglas L. Callister, "Our God Truly Is God," *Ensign*, January 2008.

49. Ibid.

50. Robert Briffault, *Rational Evolution* (New York: The Macmillan Company, 1930).

51. Richard Dawkins, CNN Television interview, September 6, 2012.

52. *Charles Darwin, The Autobiography of Charles Darwin, 1809–82*, as quoted in *The Portable Atheist*, ed. Christopher Hitchens (Boston: Da Capo Press, 2007). 94.

53. (It should be stated that many LDS scholars, along a continuum of belief and opinions on evolution, look at the irrefutable evidence discovered in the fossil record and support many of the theories of evolution.)

54. Niles Eldredge and S. J. Gould, "Punctuated equilibria: an alternative to phyletic gradualism," *Models in Paleobiology* (San Francisco: Freeman, Cooper and Company, 1972), 82–115.

55. Alfred Jarry, *Exploits and Opinions of Dr. Faustroll, Pataphysician* (Paris: Fasquelle, 1911), 114.

56. Régine Pernoud, *Joan of Arc by Herself and Her Witnesses* (Lanham: Maryland, Scarborough House, 1990).

57. Willard Trask (translator), *In Her Own Words* (New York: Turtle Point Press, 1996), 5–6.

58. Richard Swinburne, as quoted in Richard Gule, "Swinburne's Argument from Religious Experience (1994)," *Reason and the Christian Religion* (Oxford: Oxford University Press).

59. Jean-Jacques Rousseau, *Émile ou de l'Éducation* (*Émile or On Education*), 1762.

60. Kenneth Einar Himma, "Ontological Argument," *Internet Encyclopedia of Philosophy*, April 27, 2005, see http://www.iep.utm.edu/ont-arg/.

61. C. S. Lewis, *The Problem of Pain* (Oxford: Geoffrey Bles, 1940), 25.

62. William H. Drummond, *The Life of Michael Servetus* (London: John Chapman, 1848).

63. Quentin L. Cook, "Those Songs They Could Not Sing," *Ensign*, November 2011.

64. Ibid.

65. As an aside, it is doubtful that Joseph Smith, having become accustomed to religious beliefs of his day (which encompassed teachings after these plain and precious truths were omitted from scripture), believed or understood the importance of many of the teachings in the Book of Mormon—more evidence of his prophetic calling.

66. John Calvin, *Institutes of the Christian Faith* (Louisville: Westminster John Knox Press, 1960).

67. *Discourses of Wilford Woodruff* (Salt Lake City: Bookcraft, 1969), 152.

68. James E. Talmage, in Conference Report, April 1930, 97.

69. Maurice Maeterlinck, *The Blue Bird*, scene 3, "The Kingdom of the Future."

70. Ibid.

71. Amy Dempsey, "Unsung hero gave Toronto family ticket out of Nazi-occupied Austria," *The Toronto Star*, April 18, 2012.

72. "'Hotel Rwanda' Manager: We've Failed to Learn from History," *National Public Radio*, April 5, 2014.

73. Carlfred Broderick, *One Flesh, One Heart* (Salt Lake City: Deseret Book, 2010), 50–53.

74. *Teachings of the Prophet Joseph Smith*, 354.

75. *History of the Church*, ed. B. H. Roberts, 7 vols. (Salt Lake City: The Church of Jesus Christ of Latter-day Saints, 1932–51), 6:310–12.

76. *Journal of Discourses*, Vol. 10, 24.

77. C. S. Lewis, *Surprised by Joy*, 215.

78. Ibid.

79. C. S. Lewis, *Mere Christianity*, 64.

80. Dick Hoyt and Don Yaeger, *Devoted: The Story of a Father's Love for His Son* (Boston: Da Capo Press, 2012).

81. Jewish pseudepigraphical writings also known as the *Apocalypse of Moses.*

82. "Joseph Smith Letterbook 1," 1–6, as quoted in Dean Jessee, *Personal Writings of Joseph Smith* (Salt Lake City: Deseret Book, 2002).

83. Jonathan Edwards (1703–58), "Sinners in the Hands of an Angry God," selected sermon (Enfield, Connecticut, July 8, 1741).

84. John Calvin, *Institutes of the Christian Faith.*

85. George Bancroft, as quoted in Josiah Hotchkiss Gilbert, *Dictionary of Burning Words of Brilliant Writers* (New York: W. B. Ketcham, 1895), 22.

86. Richard J. Maynes, "Establishing a Christ-Centered Home," *Ensign*, May 2011.

87. Russell M. Nelson, "Thanks Be to God," *Ensign*, May 2012.

88. Joseph Smith, as quoted in Hyrum L. Andrus, *God, Man, and the Universe* (Salt Lake City: Bookcraft, 1968), 110–11.

89. William Carl Placher, *Readings in the History of Christian Theology* (Louisville: Westminster John Knox Press, 1988).

90. Jeffrey R. Holland, "The Only True God and Jesus Christ Whom He Hath Sent," *Ensign*, November 2007.

91. C. S. Lewis, *The Voyage of the Dawn Treader*, 210–11.

92. C. S. Lewis, *Miracles*, 173.

93. Bishop Richard C. Edgley, "Lessons from the Old Testament: Called of God," *Ensign*, January 2006.

94. Orson Pratt, *A[n] Interesting Account of Several Remarkable Visions* (1840).

95. *Latter-day Saints' Messenger and Advocate*, Vol. 1, 1835, 78–79.

96. Bruce R. McConkie, *The Mortal Messiah* (Salt Lake City: Deseret Book, 1980), 2:153.

97. Joseph F. Smith, *Gospel Doctrine,* 5th ed. (Salt Lake City: Deseret Book, 1939), 87–88.

98. *Teachings of the Prophet Joseph Smith*, 367.

99. *Journal of Discourses*, Vol. 26, 23.

100. Joseph Smith, *Lectures on Faith* (Salt Lake City: Deseret Book, 1985), 4:11.

101. *History of the Church*, 5:388–89.

102. David A. Bednar, "The Atonement and the Journey of Mortality," *Ensign*, April 2012.

103. J. Reuben Clark Jr., in Conference Report, September 30, 1955, 24.

104. Neal A. Maxwell, "'Willing to Submit,'" *Ensign*, May 1985, 73

105. James E. Faust, "The Atonement: Our Greatest Hope," *Ensign*, November 2001, 18.

106. George Herbert, "The Bunch of Grapes," *The Temple*, 1633.

107. Merrill J. Batemen, "The Power to Heal from Within," *Ensign*, May 1995.

108. Alma P. Burton, *Discourses of the Prophet Joseph Smith* (Salt Lake City: Deseret Book, 2011), 364.

109. Robert L. Millet, *Grace Works* (Salt Lake City: Deseret Book, 2007), 53, 61, 95.

110. Tad R. Callister, "How Can I Lead a More Saintly Life?" 89.

111. Merrill J. Batemen, "The Power to Heal from Within."

112. *Journal of Discourses*, 3:206.

113. Saint Teresa of Avila, *De Libro Vitae*, Ap. 22, 6–7, 14.

114. Jayne B. Malan, "Summer of the Lambs," *Ensign*, November 1989.

115. Lawrence E. Corbridge, "The Way," *Ensign*, November 2008.

116. *Lectures on Faith*, 5:2.

117. Ibid.

118. *Teachings of the Prophet Joseph Smith*, 220.

119. *Journal of Discourses*, 3:206.

120. *Teachings of the Prophet Joseph Smith*, 187–88.

121. *Journal of Discourses*, Vol. 9, 170.

122. C. S. Lewis, *Mere Christianity*, 174.

123. James E. Faust, "The Supernal Gift of the Atonement," *Ensign*, November 1988.

124. *Journal of Discourses*, Vol. 21, 85.

125. Ibid., Vol. 20, 187.

126. Mohandas Gandhi, *Young India*, December 31, 1931.

127. E. Stanley Jones, *Mahatma Gandhi: An Interpretation* (Charleston, South Carolina: Nabu Press, March 2014), 110.

128. Ibid.

129. *Teachings of the Prophet Joseph Smith,* 295.

130. *History of the Church*, 5:126–27.

131. Richard Lloyd Anderson, "The Alvin Smith Story: Fact and Fiction," *Ensign*, August 1987, 68–69.

132. Todd Compton, *In Sacred Loneliness* (Salt Lake City: Signature Books, December 1997), 10.

133. Hugh B. Brown, *An Abundant Life* (Salt Lake City: Signature Books, 1988), 228—quoting an article by Bonnie Chamberlin, printed in *Saturday Review.*

134. *Teachings of the Prophet Joseph Smith*, 326, 367.

135. Robert D. Richardson Jr., *Emerson: The Mind on Fire* (Oakland, California: University of California Press, November 1996), 108.

136. Ralph Waldo Emerson, *Journals and Miscellaneous Notebooks of Ralph Waldo Emerson*, Vol. IV:7, March 29, 1832.

137. Neal A. Maxwell, "'Overcome . . . Even as I Also Overcame,'" *Ensign*, May 1987.

138. John Taylor, *The Gospel Kingdom* (Salt Lake City: Deseret Book, 1987), 58.

139. John Milton, *Paradise Lost*, Book I, (Edinburgh: Samuel Simmons, 1667), Line 263.

140. Ibid., Lines 106–8.

141. Dante Alighieri, *Inferno*, "Hell" (1320).

142. Ibid., Canto I.

143. Christopher Linton, *From Eudoxus to Einstein: A History of Mathematical Astronomy* (Cambridge: Cambridge University Press, 2008). Copernicus was not the first to propose a heliocentric system; the first was Greek mathematician and astronomer Aristarchus of Samos, which Copernicus acknowledged.

144. Eric Petigura, Andrew Howard, and Geoffrey Marcy, "Prevalence of Earth-size planets orbiting Sun-like stars," *Proceedings of the National Academy of Sciences of the United States of America*, October 31, 2013.

145. C. S. Lewis, *Mere Christianity*, 49.

146. Sun Tzu, *The Art of War* (Nabla, 2010).

147. William Shakespeare, *King Lear*, Scene IV.

148. William Shakespeare, *The Merchant of Venice*, Scene III.

149. William Shakespeare, *King Lear*, Scene III.

150. *Teachings of the Prophet Joseph Smith*, 190.

151. Ibid., 207.

152. *Teachings of the Prophet Joseph Smith*, 357.

153. *Journal of Discourses*, Vol. 1, 352.

154. Orson F. Whitney, *Life of Heber C. Kimball* (Salt Lake City: Bookcraft, 1967), 132.

155. *Apocryphal Acts of the Apostles* (London: Gilbert and Rivington, 1871), 238–45.

156. Ibid.

157. Ibid.

158. Ibid.

159. Parley P. Pratt, *The Key to the Science of Theology* (Whitefish, Montana: Kessinger Publishing, 1998), 51.

160. Ibid.

161. *Teachings of the Prophet Joseph Smith*, 354.

162. Bruce R. McConkie, *The Mortal Messiah*, 1:23.

163. Ibid.

164. *History of the Church*, Vol. 6, 307–8.

165. John Taylor, "Origin, Object, and Destiny of Women," *Young Woman's Journal*, Vol. 8, June 1897, 411–13.

166. *Teaching of the Prophet Joseph Smith*, 357.

167. Th. Flournoy, *Philosophy of William James* (Charleston, South Carolina: BiblioBazaar, 2009), 130.

168. *History of the Church*, 4:358.

169. As related by Dr. John M. Bernhisel and reported in R. C. Gemmell, "Early History of the Medical Profession in Utah: Biography of Dr. W. F. Anderson," typewritten manuscript, Church Historian's Library, Salt Lake City, Utah, 8–11.

170. B. H. Roberts, *Scriptural Notebook*, Brigham Young University, Harold B. Lee Library, Special Collections under "F."

171. *Journal of John Whitaker*, April 6, 1894.

172. Marcel Proust, as quoted in Gabriel Marcel, *Homo Viator* (New York: Harper and Row, 1963), 8.

173. "Oh My Father," *Hymns*, no. 292.

174. Alexander Gilchrist, *The Life of William Blake*, Vol. 1 (London: Macmillan and Co., 1880), 150.

175. Thomas Traherne, "The Salutation," as quoted in *The Cambridge History of English Literature*, Vol. 7 (Cambridge: Cambridge University Press, 1911), 43.

176. Neal A. Maxwell, "Patience," BYU devotional, November 27, 1979.

177. Quoted by Truman G. Madsen, "Oh How We Know," BYU devotional, September 20, 1994.

178. Joseph F. Smith, *Gospel Doctrine*, 13–14.

179. Neal A. Maxwell, "Premortality, a Glorious Reality," *Ensign*, November 1985.

180. Orson Pratt, *The Great First Cause* (Liverpool: R. James, January 1851), 14.

181. Garland E. Tickemyer, "Joseph Smith and Process Theology," *Dialogue: A Journal of Mormon Thought* 17 (1984), 82.

182. *Teachings of the Prophet Joseph Smith*, 210.

183. *History of the Church,* Vol. 6, 312.

184. B. H. Roberts, *Comprehensive History of The Church of Jesus Christ of Latter-day Saints*, Vol. 2 (Provo, Utah: Brigham Young University Press, 1965), 399.

185. Donald Q. Cannon and Larry E. Dahl, *Encyclopedia of Joseph Smith's Teachings* (Salt Lake City: Deseret Book, 2015), 436.

186. Spencer W. Kimball, "Privileges and Responsibilities of Sisters," *Ensign*, November 1978, 105.

187. *Journal of Discourses*, Vol. 23, 368.

188. John Milton, *Paradise Lost*, Book IV, Line 319.

189. David Olsen, *The Garden Gate* (currently unpublished).

190. Dallin H. Oaks, "The Great Plan of Happiness," *Ensign*, November 1993.

191. *History of the Church*, Vol. 1, 283.

192. *Lectures on Faith*, No. 2.

193. Orson Pratt, *A[n] Interesting Account of Several Remarkable Visions.*

194. *Lectures on Faith*, No. 2.

195. Ibid.

196. Rutherford Hayes Platt, *The Forgotten Books of Eden* (Royersford, PA: Alpha House, 1927), chapter XIV.

197. Ibid., chapter XXXVIII.

198. Bruce C. Hafen, *The Broken Heart* (Salt Lake City, Deseret Book, 2008), 39.

199. Hugh Nibley, "Not to Worry," *Expressions of Faith: Testimonies of Latter-day Saint Scholars* (Salt Lake City: Deseret Book, 1996), 151.

200. Lord Byron, "Cain, a Mystery," 140.

201. Boyd K. Packer, "To Young Women and Men," *Ensign*, May 1989.

202. C. S. Lewis, *The Weight of Glory*, 9.

203. William Shakespeare, *As You Like It*, Act II, Scene VII.

204. Ibid.

205. Anatole France, *Le Crime de Sylvestre Bonnard* (Calmann Levy, 1881), Part II, chapter 4.

206. William Shakespeare, *Macbeth*, Act 5, Scene 5, 19–28.

207. Neal A. Maxwell, *The Neal A. Maxwell Quote Book* (Salt Lake City: Bookcraft, 2001), 264.

208. Allen E. Bergin, *Eternal Values and Personal Growth* (Provo, Utah: Brigham Young University Press, 2002), 4.

209. Ibid., 6.

210. Ibid., ix.

211. W. B. Yeats, "When You Are Old," *The Collected Poems of W. B. Yeats* (New York: Scribner, 1989).

212. Karl Marx, as quoted in A. M. McKinnon, "Reading 'Opium of the People': Expression, Protest and the Dialectics of Religion," *Critical Sociology*, Vol. 31, no. 1–2, 15–38.

213. John Galbraith Simmons, *The Scientific 100: A Ranking of the Most Influential Scientists, Past and Present* (New York: Citadel Press, 2000).

214. Frank E. Manuel, *The Religion of Isaac Newton* (Oxford: Oxford University Press, 1974).

215. Ibid.

216. Philip N. Moore, as quoted in *The End of History: Messiah Conspiracy* (Atlanta: RamsHead Press, 1996), 496.

217. Alfred North Whitehead, *Adventures of Ideas* (New York: Free Press, 1967), 33.

218. Owen Chadwick, *Western Asceticism* (Louisville: Westminster John Knox Press, 1958), 235.

219. Thomas Aquinas, *The Summa Theologica* III, Question 94, Article 1.

220. Sermon delivered at Nauvoo, Illinois., August 15, 1840 (source: "Reminiscent Account of Simon Baker," *Journal History*, LDS Archives).

221. Friedrich Nietzsche, *The Gay Science* (1882), Section 125.

222. David V. Dearden, "The Sacred Gift of Agency, Choice, and Decisions," BYU devotional, March 31, 2009.

223. Steven Crowell, "Existentialism," *Stanford Encyclopedia of Philosophy*, March 9, 2015.

224. Alan Pratt defined existential nihilism as "the notion that life has no intrinsic meaning or value, and it is, no doubt, the most commonly used and understood sense of the word today" (see *Internet Encyclopedia of Philosophy*).

225. *Journal of Discourses*, Vol. 11, 375.

226. *History of the Church*, 4:540.

227. Spencer W. Kimball, in Conference Report, April 1964, 93–94.

228. Sigmund Freud, *The Future of an Illusion* (London: Hogarth Press, 1927), chapters VII and VIII.

229. C. S. Lewis, "The Seeing Eye," *Christian Reflections* (Grand Rapids, Michigan: Wm. B. Eerdmans Publishing, 1967), 167.

230. Jeffrey R. Holland, "Prophet's, Seers, and Revelators," *Ensign*, November 2004.

231. The following excerpts from Lewis and Freud are quoted in Armand Nicholi, *The Question of God: Sigmund Freud & C. S. Lewis* (New York: Free Press, 2004) .

232. Ibid.

233. Ibid.

234. C. S. Lewis, *Mere Christianity*.

235. Robert Louis Stevenson, *Familiar Studies of Men and Books* (Claremont, California: Pomona Press, 1882).

236. See James E. Faust, "Them That Honour Me I Will Honour," *Ensign*, May 2001.

237. C. S. Lewis, *Surprised by Joy*, 215.

238. "Oh My Father," *Hymns*, no. 292.

239. Richard C. Galbraith, *Scriptural Annotations and Introduction*, selected and arranged by Joseph Fielding Smith, 60.

240. *Lectures on Faith*, 5:3d.

241. C. S. Lewis, *Miracles,* 93–94.

242. Jack London, *Jack London's Tales of Adventure*, ed. Irving Shepard (New York: Doubleday, 1960), vii.

About the Author

David Olsen has served as a bishop and early morning seminary teacher, where he developed his love for searching the scriptures, as well as the revelations and teachings of the Prophet Joseph Smith. He is the president of Market Builders, a national public relations and marketing agency. He is also the author of the bestselling references books *The Words You Should Know* and *801 Things You Should Know*. He and his wife, Holly, are the proud parents of five children. David blogs at www.MySoulHungered.com.

SCAN to visit

WWW.MYSOULHUNGERED.COM

0 26575 17222 5